"Developing Christ-like care in our churches serves so many ambitions. It blesses those inside the church who receive that care, and it commends Christ to those outside the church who see the quality of the care being given. Helen Thorne-Allenson's book is a faithful, biblical and comprehensive guide to the principles and practicalities of being a caring church. Broad in scope yet detailed in application, this book will help all our churches grow the kind of caring culture that is both glorifying and obedient to Christ."

**Steve Midgley,** Executive Director, BCUK; Author, *Understanding Trauma*

"Wanting a church that cares and having a church that cares are two different things. Helen both identifies the barriers to the practice of authentic care and offers realistic strategies to growing both the desire and the capability within yourself and others. Reading and discussing this book together would be an ideal way for your church to grow in care through inviting and encouraging every member to play their part."

**Andrew King,** Association Secretary, Grace Baptist Churches South East, UK

"In this accessible and practical book, Helen gives us a hope-filled and Bible-saturated yet realistic vision for churches that care well. I am confident it will be a stimulating and encouraging resource for anyone who wants to help their church grow in this vital area, whether a church leader or a member of the congregation. It is a great place to start!"

**Kerstin Bowsher,** Church Pastoral Worker, Grace Church, Porthcawl, Wales

"Helen skilfully and gently shows us, in a practical and accessible way, how we can build and nurture a culture of biblical care in our churches. I felt genuinely cared for as I read. It is a must-read for anyone passionate about helping people grow and pointing them to Jesus."

**Fernanda Curtis,** Women's Worker, Christ Church Cambourne, near Cambridge, UK

"Love is patient, love is kind… and church is messy. This book gets that. Gospel-centred and pastorally sensitive, it speaks to churches of all shapes and sizes, and paints a picture of what it looks like when we learn how to love one another. It will challenge and encourage you in equal measure with lots of practical ideas for growing a culture of care. Well worth reading!"

**Matt Beeby,** Rector, St James' Church, Gerrards Cross, Bucks, UK

"I am so grateful for this book and will be reading it regularly for years to come. It has challenged me to be more imaginative in prayer for my church, more diligent in my love for others, and more proactively collaborative in creating a culture of care. Helen's writing is thoroughly biblical and wonderfully realistic; she consistently sets a vision for growth which is exciting, challenging and Christ-honouring, yet does so with humility and gentleness, using relatable examples."

**Eleanor Godwin,** Pastoral Worker, St Giles' Church, Derby, UK

"Once again, Helen has written clearly and biblically with wisdom and compassion born of faithful gospel application in the nuances of everyday life and of the wealth of experience which that brings. Whether you read this by yourself, with a friend, in a small group or as a whole church, this book will help you live out Jesus' command to love one another just as he loves us and, in doing so, to show the world that we are his disciples."

**Helen Morrow,** Assistant Pastor, Holy Trinity Church, West Bromwich, UK; Tutor, BCUK Foundations Course

"I loved this book! Helen's understanding of people and experience of being part of a local church for many years are so evident throughout, and I frequently found myself thinking, 'You know my heart, and you know my church'. She is wonderfully realistic about the challenges we face when it comes to loving one another well but left me feeling excited that we really can make progress, and that our culture can change, as we acknowledge our need and look to Christ."

**Andrea Trevenna,** Women's Minister, St Nicholas' Church, Sevenoaks, Kent, UK

"Wise, practical, challenging and motivating, Helen's book has fuelled my love for my local church and spurred me on to love others well. Anyone who serves in any way in their church should read this book. The wonderfully rich application of Scripture, alongside 'how-tos', FAQs, training outlines and lived examples, invites discussion, reflection, personal change and action. I can't wait to read it with others in the ministry contexts I serve in and see how God uses it to change our hearts, our prayers and our church care."

**Esther Lynch,** Irish Church Missions churches, Dublin; Team Lead, Equipped to Care, Ireland

"Helen draws on a wealth of experience in helping both individuals and churches grow in their ability to care well for one another. Each chapter is accessible yet packed full of biblical encouragement, practical application, inspiring stories and challenging questions. Aimed at equipping both leaders and congregation members, this book is an invaluable resource, whether read individually or within a small group, ministry team or whole church."

**Dr Joanna Jackson,** Counselling Psychologist; former Director of Counselling, All Souls Church Langham Place, London

"How different are our Christian communities? Surely an acid test is how well we love and care for our brothers and sisters, and particularly for those who are in pain or vulnerable. Helen has given us such a helpful book to encourage us to do this like Jesus—thoughtfully and humbly. I wish I'd had this book years ago. There is much wisdom to help me, and the church family, to care like Jesus more and more."

**Rachel Meynell,** Minister for Pastoral Care, St Mary's Church Maidenhead, Berkshire, UK

# A CHURCH THAT CARES

*A Biblical Guide to Loving One Another Well*

Helen Thorne-Allenson

thegoodbook COMPANY

Published by:
The Good Book Company

thegoodbook.com | thegoodbook.co.uk
thegoodbook.com.au | thegoodbook.co.nz



Every book published by The Good Book Company has been written by a human author and edited by a human editor. While AI tools are sometimes used to assist with research and support certain processes, all content has been created by a human author and thoroughly checked by our editorial team to ensure it is biblically faithful and pastorally wise.



Design by Ben Woodcraft

A CIP catalogue record for this book is available from the British Library.

ISBN: 9781802544015 | JOB-008620 | Printed in India

# CONTENTS

# INTRODUCTION

If there is one thing I have learned from my recent renewed foray into gardening, it is that nothing grows well unless it is tended. Things do grow without help—that is for sure—but what grows, and how it grows, is very much dependent on the care the plants are given. Left to its own devices, a vegetable patch quickly becomes full of weeds. Without the proper care, the runner beans intertwine with the tomatoes and quickly form a cat's cradle of greenery that distorts both plants. If not picked in time, the fresh vegetables become rotten vegetables. And don't get me started on caterpillars and the havoc they can wreak... Gardens need tending if they are to flourish and be fruitful.

Churches are a lot like gardens. A culture will always grow—an approach to caring for others will always emerge. But what that culture is and how it functions will depend on the kind of nurturing the church has been given: the sort of teaching they have received, the kind of role-modelling that has been displayed, and the quality of relationships that have been grown. A flourishing culture will not just appear by accident or simply come to pass because gospel truth is proclaimed with gentleness. If we want our churches to overflow with the love of Christ in ways that encourage people to come to Christ and grow in Christ, in all seasons of life, there needs to be an intentionality in tending that growth. Without it, love and care can get muddled or muted or pushed to one side.

What follows in this book does not set out everything that we might need to know in order to grow a culture of love and care for one another well. It is far from comprehensive. But what it does aim to do is to set out what a culture of Christ-like care might look like in a local church and suggest a range of areas to attend to in order to grow and maintain that culture and care. Some of those areas may seem obvious and some may take you by surprise, but hopefully all will feel achievable over time. And all require each of us—leaders and congregation members alike—to be involved.

Thankfully this work does not rely on us alone. We can be confident that the Lord is always at work in his church, growing what is good—we simply need to follow his lead and avoid pulling in a different direction. And as we seek to be faithful to God's call to love one another well, we can enjoy reaping the wonderful fruits—comfort, hope, encouragement, sanctification and witness—that flow from a church that loves and cares like Christ.

It is my hope and prayer that, as you read, you will become ever more excited about God's call to love others well and will know the blessing of the Lord as you engage in his work of caring for others, in his church, for his eternal glory.

> *"Praise be to the God and Father of our Lord Jesus Christ, the Father of compassion and the God of all comfort, who comforts us in all our troubles, so that we can comfort those in any trouble with the comfort we ourselves receive from God." (2 Corinthians 1:3-4)*

SECTION 1

# PRINCIPLES OF CARING WELL

# CHAPTER 1

# CALL: WHY CARING MATTERS

"Love one another deeply, from the heart" (1 Peter 1:22). So wrote the apostle Peter to the early church. The apostle Paul instructed the believers with whom he was in contact in a similar vein: "Be devoted to one another" (Romans 12:10), and, "Serve one another humbly in love" (Galatians 5:13), he said. The apostle John agreed with them both: "I ask that we love one another" (2 John 5), he penned. The point is obvious: love is meant to be central to all Christians say and do.

Such teaching is rooted in the person and work of Christ. Jesus expressed extraordinary love when he left the glories of heaven to be incarnated as a man. Jesus modelled counter-cultural care and kindness during his earthly ministry: touching the "unclean" (Mark 1:41); speaking with the outcasts (John 4); calling those who had made serious mistakes to follow him (Mark 2:13-17). And then Jesus displayed the pinnacle of love as he hung on the cross, taking the sins of the world on his shoulders so people like us can go free, clothed with his robes of righteousness. Jesus, as God, embodies love. It is not just what he shows; it is who he is. God is love (1 John 4:8).

No wonder, then, that he taught his followers to love. "As I have loved you, so you must love one another," he said (John 13:34). The greatest commandments given are to love God wholeheartedly and love one another deeply (Matthew

22:36-40). One of the hallmarks of the Christian church should be love—so much so that in his *Apology* (chapter 39), the early Christian theologian Tertullian wrote of the Christian church, "See how they love one another". In a believing community, love should be startling and obvious.

## Love that makes a difference

It is a beautiful thing when an ethos of love is at the core of a local congregation. Beautiful because it is an expression of obedience to Christ. Beautiful because it is a powerful witness to an unbelieving world. Beautiful because it is a sign that Christians are being who they are designed to be, living in ways that encourage one another to flourish in the faith. Beautiful because it is an act of worship—a hallmark of being a set-apart people who seek to live lives worthy of our calling (Ephesians 4:1).

Love is an intensely practical characteristic, and it is one that works itself out in the care of others. Love means that people will feel able to and be wanting to share their lives, not just the gospel, as Paul did with the Thessalonian church (1 Thessalonians 2:8). Loves means that people will experience freedom to be honest about the ups and downs of life, knowing that those around them will respond by rejoicing with those who rejoice and weeping with those who weep (Romans 12:15). Love gives people the courage to bring dark things into the light, confident that as they speak of their battle with sin, they will be met with humility and grace and pointed back to the Father, who loves to welcome them home (Luke 15:11-32). Love propels believers to set aside selfish ambition and genuinely want what is best for those around them (Philippians 2:3-8). Love spurs people on to growth in Christ-likeness (Ephesians 3:17-19).

We see the faithful nature of that love in the story of a woman with a chronic illness, often unable to leave the family home, who was regularly visited, cared for and prayed for by her church family over many years. The fact she could not get out and could not serve on Sundays did not diminish the ways in which she was valued and included in the body of Christ. Meals were prepared, time was spent with her, biblical encouragement was shared, and songs were listened to together until she went home to be with the Lord.

We see the transformational nature of that love in the story of an older man who had been addicted to alcohol for many years, who was welcomed into the local church. He had pushed so many people away over the years. His family had long given up on him—they could not take his lies and outbursts any longer—but the care of Christ and his community gradually broke through. As this man was loved, he saw the power of the cross, and he began to believe that change was actually possible. He learned to be honest, he learned to find other ways of dealing with the pain, and he learned to live a truly loving life, even able to reach out to his children once more and genuinely ask for their forgiveness.

We see the compassionate nature of love in the story of a woman who was bereaved in her early 30s, her husband taken in a tragic car accident. Left to bring up her three young children by herself, she must have felt as if her life had come crashing down—but her church family rallied round. Life was done together: school runs, shopping, play dates and parenting decisions all became things she could do with others when she wanted the support. She had friends to cry with, to talk with, to pray with and to grow with. The church cared, and she and her kids thrived.

We see the gracious nature of love in the story of the young man who was battling sporadic pornography use. He never had to labour under the impression that he was the only one struggling that way, because the church was open about the reality that lots of men (and women) experience pornography's lure. There was a grace-based structure for him to seek help within the congregation. No additional guilt or shame was piled on him—just a consistent, caring encouragement to look to Christ for freedom and hope.

We see the quiet nature of love in the story of a young couple trying to work out how to do life together. No one imposed rules upon them, but there were multiple couples within the church who were willing to listen and share wisdom with them. When it came to finances, decision-making, diary planning and sex, there were people who would simply listen, pray and encourage them to live for Christ day by day. Love propelled the community to love the couple well.

We see the strength of love in the young man who was starting out in the workplace and constantly feeling the pressure to compromise his faith (or, at the very least, hide it). Among his peers, there was always some coarse joking and some pressure to lie to get ahead. He could so easily have joined in had it not been for the regular encouragement of his small group. They didn't come up with trite platitudes. They didn't merely tell him to stand firm. They heard the complexity; they saw the depth of temptation—and they prayed. They gently talked through how he might respond in the hard situations he faced. They loved him on the days he got it wrong. They showed him what it is to live life humbly yet faithfully before an unbelieving world.

We see the wise nature of love in the nurturing of a woman who was doubting her faith. She was given space to articulate her concerns: she knew she would not be condemned for asking questions and that it was safe to bring her queries to her church and the Lord. The leaders committed to regular meetings with her. They listened, they discussed, and they spotted the underlying fears as well as hearing the surface questions about the sovereignty of God. She was given space to explore Scripture alongside friends over a significant period of time. And they cared, so they did not give up praying, even when she temporarily walked away.

We see the unexpected humility of love when a man who had begun controlling his wife—expecting her to do his bidding and to live life in obedience to his desires—began to see the damage he had done to his family. Instead of making excuses or covering it up, he was won over by the culture of repentance in the church. Little by little he saw that his reluctance to admit his faults went against the grain of Christian living. He began to see that the marriages around him, in which the husbands were humble and gentle and quick to put their family above their reputations, were the ones that were flourishing. And when he finally admitted the horrors of his idol of control and sought help, he came to taste a personal freedom and a depth of connection with those around him that he had never known before. His family were able to thrive once more.

Love really does change everything.

## Love that struggles

Caring is not easy though. Love is much harder to grow and maintain in a congregation than we might like to admit. And, if we take an honest look at our church communities, we will see there is some growing to be done. Often, the trouble is that caring for those around us has fallen off the priority list. No church would say it is unimportant, but an intentionality about nurturing it has been swamped by other things.

Sometimes love has been pushed aside as doctrinal battles have been fought. Churches have been embroiled in denominational disputes, the authority of Scripture has been undermined, and the priority has been to fight for what is right. People have been encouraged to prioritise truth—to make sure every theological i is dotted and t is crossed—and the deep relational culture of the church has, at times, been sacrificed. Care never stands in opposition to truth. Indeed, love rejoices in truth (1 Corinthians 13:6). But love is essential. Without it, anything else we may do, even the defence of Scriptural authority, is nothing more than a "clanging cymbal"—a blunt sound that brings no pleasure to the Lord.

Sometimes love has been pushed aside by pain and suffering. For some, the church has been a place of deep and profound hurt. A few leaders have crushed their congregation members. A few congregation members have crushed their leaders. Cultures that have previously been accepted as normal have come to be seen to be broken in the extreme. Some have got scared. Self-protection has become the order of the day. Keeping others at arm's length has felt like the more sensible course to keep further suffering at bay.

Sometimes love has been pushed aside because it is just hard. As Christians, we may be united by Christ, but we are a diverse community. Our temperaments, preferences on secondary issues and passions for different areas of ministry vary. It is easier to follow your own path than come together in an attitude of Christ-like compassion and care. We have sometimes allowed churches to become places of individual expression rather than corporate care.

And in the process, we have seen some of the rotten fruits of those tendencies. We see it in the stories of the individuals with chronic illness who were effectively abandoned by the church save for the occasional email check-in, because it was too hard to keep visiting someone who is not improving health-wise and is never going to be able to "contribute" to the work. We see it in the stories of alcoholics left on the periphery because it felt awkward and uncomfortable and a bit messy to get involved, and so no one stepped forward. We see it in the stories of the bereaved, whose non-Christian friends provide so much more support than the busy friends at church. We see it in those young people struggling with pornography who keep their battles silent because they have no evidence that their stories will be treated with care. We see it in the young couples who labour under the burdensome impression that they really ought to be able to work out this marriage thing alone, and who spend years quietly drifting apart before a crisis appears that leaves everyone around them stunned. We see it in the individuals living double lives, smiling sweetly on a Sunday but acting abominably on a Monday. We see it in the lives of those who have walked away from the church because they didn't feel able to bring their doubts to their brothers and sisters in Christ—or because, when they did, they were met with a simplistic download of truth that completely missed their confusion and fears. We see it in the lives of those people who know they are treating their family awfully but are so terrified of having to admit they are wrong, with the reputational risk which that brings, that the whole family stays trapped until someone walks away.

When we fail to care for one another in the way that Jesus commands, people in our churches are left broken, reeling and alone.

## Love that is observed

It is not just within the church that the presence or absence of a culture of care leaves its mark. Those outside the church are impacted too. Acts 2 reminds us that it is as the church meets, devotes itself to Scripture (v 42) and shares with and cares for one another well (v 44) that it grows. The world watches Christians. When it sees superficiality, partiality, pride, arrogance, lack of integrity and other unloving attitudes, the church is seen to be falling very far short of what they are designed to be. On the other hand, when the watching world sees love and care, and the Spirit's work in enabling people to love like that, that is attractive indeed.

The only reason why I went to church as a young adult was because I saw extraordinary love in a couple of people there. They were not perfect, but they were kind, sacrificial, generous, hospitable, willing to apologise when they got things wrong, patient and persevering—they chose to love me when I was deeply unlovely. Of course, the Holy Spirit was the one who ultimately opened my eyes to the gospel, but it was the deep care of Christians who commended that gospel to me.

Since becoming a Christian, I have known the ups and downs of church life. I have been loved. I have been treated unlovingly. I have loved. I have acted unlovingly. And, in each of those circumstances, I have seen the consequences, both delightful and desperate, of the presence or absence of a culture of love and care.

I imagine it is the same for you. As you have read this chapter, I hope there have been stories of love flooding your mind: moments when you have seen the difference care has made to your story of coming to Christ and growing in him. I am conscious that there may also be stories of lack of love gripping your heart: stories where you or someone you care about has been sidelined or hurt in ways that are really painful to recall. Stories where your faith journey has been marred by a culture that is very far from loving and kind.

This book is designed to enable you, whoever you are, to play your part in helping your church grow so that the stories of flourishing far outnumber the stories of pain. As we go through the chapters ahead, we will begin to see more of what this culture of love and care looks like. We will wrestle more deeply with the obstacles that get in the way. And we will look at how to help our church flourish—whether we are young or old, male or female, in leadership or just new to faith.

One day, the church will be perfect. We will be perfect people, in a perfect place, gathered around the perfect throne of Christ (1 John 3:1-3; Revelation 21 – 22). But in this life, our churches will never be perfect. Yet, as we pursue love together, we will become ever more the worshipping community we are designed to be.

## Questions for reflection

1. What excites you about God's call to love and care for others well?
2. To what extent is love on view in your local church? Note and thank God for some specific examples of where love has shone out.
3. In what ways is (or can) pastoral care be something that helps your church reach out to those who do not yet know Christ?

CHAPTER 2

# CULTURE: WHAT CARE LOOKS LIKE

The vision of a church that cares is an exciting one. What wonderful fruit can be displayed in the lives of believers when we work together as we are designed to. What a wonderful witness to those not in the church and what a powerful way to display God's glory day by day. I hope you want to be more a church where those kinds of outcomes are seen. But what kind of church do we need to be to see that happen? What would it take for people to see others loved that well? Or, to put it in more biblical language, what does it look like to live a life worthy of our calling (Ephesians 4:1)?

In this chapter we are going to look at six distinctives, all drawn from Ephesians 4—six aspects of healthy caring church culture (our shared attitudes, values, actions and approach to being a church together) that will shine like a light in a dark world. These distinctives are not exhaustive; there are other areas we could explore. But these are six areas that, when working well, can enable our churches to flourish in their love and care.

## A gentle humility: where people know each other and bear with each other

If you were Paul, writing to the church in Ephesus to set out what living a life worthy of their calling looks like, where would you start?

- Gospel truth? Certainly foundational.
- Passion for evangelism? Clearly essential.
- Pursuit of purity? The Bible affirms the importance of this time and again.

Each of those things is explored by Paul—indeed, each is affirmed by Paul as absolutely integral to the Christian life, but, when it comes to living a life worthy of our calling, he starts somewhere else. He starts this section of his letter by encouraging the Ephesians to be humble, gentle and patient (Ephesians 4:2). What an extraordinary calling! Yes, we need to believe what is right, and, yes, we need to reach out with passion, and, yes, we need to pursue personal holiness. But when it comes to church, to be humble (dependent on the Lord and thinking of others before ourselves), patient (being slow to anger and willing to do life together long term, even when that is hard) and gentle (treating everyone with loving kindness, knowing they are precious to the Lord and struggling with the pain of this fallen world) will be our duty and our joy.

Paul knows that we worship the God who is slow to anger and abounding in love (Exodus 34:6-7). Therefore, for us to be imitators of God must mean that our relationships will be typified by great patience with one another: no bickering, irritability or a desire to brush others aside. God knows we have been rescued by the Saviour who was willing to leave the glories of heaven, empty himself, and serve us in our need (Philippians 2:6-11). So, for us to be imitators of Christ must mean that our relationships in the church will shine out with a desire to serve one another. There should be no superstars who shirk washing up, no in-crowd and out, no seeking advancement or prestige—but rather a deep humility that consistently puts others first. Paul knows we have no reason to boast in anything other than Christ (Galatians 6:14). So, as the Spirit works in us, we will gradually come to see that there can be no looking down on others and that there is no reason to think we are better than others.

Within a culture like this, it is safe to share because there are no cliques, no power plays and no desire to keep anyone in their place but just a deep desire to love each other and see each other flourish in faith. People will not fear vulnerability because they know their sin and suffering will never be used against them in vengeful ways. There may be moments when justice needs to be sought because of someone's serious sin, but, even then, they will receive the help they need to persevere and become more like Christ. Members will not fear weakness because everyone acknowledges their utter dependence on Christ, and asking each other for help will be the most natural thing in the world. Each week, humility, gentleness and patience will be clear.

Note that Paul is not writing the letter to some kind of perfect church where it is really easy to bear with one another and humbly serve. This was no highly sanctified grouping where no one wound anyone up. In Ephesians 4:31 these believers are told to get rid of all bitterness and rage, which implies there was a fair bit of bitterness and rage going around. Paul was calling imperfect Christians in an imperfect church to be gentle, humble and patient, because that is what God's love should look like in a church if it is a truly loving and caring place to be. What a call!

### A real unity: where people from all backgrounds are equal and do life together

A second distinctive of a church where members are living lives worthy of their calling is unity. This is the kind of unity that comes when God brings together people from all kinds of backgrounds through Jesus' wonderful work on the cross.

It's a unity that flows from a deep desire to put into practice the kind of humility we have just been looking at above—unity that is rooted in being willing to associate with people from all walks of life (Romans 12:16).

In Ephesians 2, Paul reflects that in the world there are fault lines between people groups. For him and the Ephesian church, the headline division was between Jews and Gentiles—two groups who would never give each other the time of day. But now, in Christ, that dividing wall has come down (v 14). Through Jesus' sacrifice and victory over death, enemies become friends—in fact they become closer than friends; they become one. And what a beautiful unity that is: people from every background joining together, worshipping one Lord, sharing one baptism and having the privilege of being loved by one Father (4:5-6).

Your church probably doesn't suffer from fault lines as deep as the division between Jews and Gentiles in the 1st century, but many churches have people who fit and people who do not. Maybe the division lies in ethnicity, between those who are from the dominant culture and those who are not. Maybe it lies in education, between those who are book people or degree people and those who are not. Maybe it lies in music, between those who are "moving with the times" and those who are steeped in tradition. Maybe it lies in financial standing, between those who can give abundantly to the work of mission or spend plenty on their families and those who cannot. Diversity is beautiful, but divisions between different people should be utterly alien to the church. Our calling is to something so much better: to be a people, to be a community where all are welcome, where all are equal, where all are valued and where all play an essential part in the body.

## A passion for equipping: where all grow their distinct gifts for service

That equality will show itself, in part, in a deep desire to help everyone grow the gifts that God has given them and help everyone flourish in service within the local church (Ephesians 4:7). The Lord is so very generous with his gifts. By his Spirit he enables some to teach, others to lead, still more to encourage… the list is long. And he does not leave anyone out. Indeed, there is no such thing as a Christian who has no gifts. Everyone has something which the Lord has carefully chosen for them so that they can bless others in the church.

None of the gifts are more important than the others. All are essential. An eye cannot say to a hand that it's not needed (1 Corinthians 12:21). So, part of being a church that is living a life worthy of our calling is being a place where people know what their gifts are, people are encouraged to develop those gifts, and people are encouraged to use those gifts in the service of the church. Indeed, one of the main roles of a church leader is to help equip believers for works of service (Ephesians 4:12): to know and grow their God-given gifts so that the church can be the place of love that it is designed to be. What value and purpose people will know when the church functions in this way.

It is probably worth adding a few caveats. There are seasons when even the most abundantly gifted person may need to step back from service. If sin or suffering get the upper hand, sometimes a season away from service is good. I have taken a few breaks here and there when life has been particularly hard. There are times in local church life when we may need to do things that we do not feel particularly gifted at. I remember being a music director in a small church for a season. I was not very good at it, but there were not many musicians in our plant, and so I dusted off my rusty piano skills and gave it a go. And there are moments in the local church when someone will display a gift that we are not quite sure what to do with. Sometimes it takes time and creativity to see how gifts might be put to good in God's kingdom, and, at times like that, we may need to move slowly in new directions to ensure ministry activities are sustainable. But a church that is functioning well will be a place where everyone is constantly on the lookout for how God is gifting his children and is keen to help those gifts flourish through service.

## A desire for maturity: where the gospel makes a difference—past, present and future

Gifts are not given or grown just for the pleasure of individual Christians. We do not help each other identify our gifts and serve so we can find ways to indulge our own particular ministry passions or hobby-horse. Our gifts are given so we can help each other mature (Ephesians 4:13). Like a good parent who is committed to seeing their child fed and nurtured from birth until that day they pass their driving test, get the keys to their new home and buy their first DIY kit from the local hardware store, in the church we are called to help people delight more and more in Jesus each day and grow to be more and more like him.

Every time we meet, we have the opportunity to look forward to the future. And when we do, we are caring for others. When suffering is overwhelming, we can remind each other that the pain is only temporary. When there is injustice, we can enable each other to hold on to the fact that one day justice will absolutely be done. When sickness takes hold, we can point each other to the ultimate healing that comes when Jesus returns and, in the blink of an eye, we will be in a place of no more sickness, no more pain and no more tears (Revelation 21:4).

However, the gospel is so much more than an antidote to the problems of the past and a promise of the perfection to come. In the gospel, there is hope for today. In our anxiety, depression, grief, addiction, stress, miscarriage, childlessness, marriage strife or abuse, we can help each other engage with the God who speaks, the God who is active, the God who never sleeps. One of the great callings of Christ's church is to be a place where we can say to each other, "Look to Jesus—he is working right now, and he is good".

## A preparation for suffering: where there is commitment to walk alongside each other

We do not need to wait until hard times come before we talk about God's great help and hope in times of trouble. We have the privilege of being people who help each other prepare for the tough times so that when they do hit (and they will), we are people who can stand firm.

I have some large trees in my front garden, each standing about 70 feet high. As I look out of my window, the wind is whipping round them, but they are standing firm. Their roots are deep and their trunks are strong. They are not going anywhere in a storm. Our calling is to help our brothers and sisters grow strong too. Not to escape storms nor to be unaffected by storms (there are plenty of leaves falling off my trees)—but to be people who can avoid being tossed around by false teachers, people who pressure them or people who wound (Ephesians 4:14). Our calling is to help one another come through the storms still standing, still with our eyes on Christ.

That cannot be achieved through listening to a few talks here and there. That kind of deep rootedness will never come about by understanding alone. That is the kind of depth of maturity that comes through a lifetime of walking alongside each other saying, "Let's remember..." "Let's pray..." "Let's trust…" "Let's lift our eyes…" "Let's lament…" and "Let's persevere…" We can help each other grow strong and ready for whatever the Lord brings into our lives.

### A commitment to wise speech: where people are encouraged and pointed to Christ

A great deal of the privileges we have been exploring in this chapter come about as we speak with one another—as we speak the truth in love, to be precise (Ephesians 4:15). By ensuring that everything we say when we meet as church (whether from the front or in conversations) is both true and loving, we can help each other become more confident in Christ.

It is dangerous to miss either part of that pairing. To be untrue is to dishonour the Lord, to lead others astray, to leave those around us unequipped to live their lives in community well. To be unloving is to dishonour the Lord, to risk damaging those who are already bruised and to reduce God to a set of doctrines rather than remember that he is a Father who speaks tenderly to those in his care.

As we speak to one another in truth and love, we can help each other change. Churches are designed to be places where we transform together. Places where we help each other take off our old desires and behaviours and put on new ways of thinking and living as our hearts are conformed more to the likeness of Christ (v 22-24). Places where we mature in our understanding, attitudes and ways of behaving. Places where we learn to process the pain of life and grow in perseverance. Places where we move away from sin and move towards godliness. Places where we spur each other on to love and good works and become ever more the community God has called us to be.

What an extraordinary calling we have! The future of our churches lies in each of us being ever more conformed to Christ in each of these areas. And as that happens, we become increasingly loving and caring communities, centred on the Christ who so loves and cares for us.

## Questions for reflection

1. Which of these characteristics do you think your church is strongest in? Praise the Lord for those things.
2. How would you like your church to grow? How can you encourage yourself—and those around you—to pray for that growth passionately and regularly?
3. Read Ephesians 4. If you are a leader, how are you equipping the saints for works of service? If you are a member, how are you speaking the truth in love with those around you in order to help them mature?

# CHAPTER 3

# STRUGGLE: WHY IT CAN BE HARD TO CARE WELL

However much we might like (or at least assent to) the idea that the church should be a place of care and unity where we are all invested in using our gifts with humility to help others grow, change and persevere, many of us find it hard. Both on a personal and a corporate level, there is something about our calling in this area that seems so very tricky. The outcomes of chapter 1 are beautiful, but the responsibilities of chapter 2 can feel very much out of reach.

Why do we struggle in this God-given calling? Meet eight fictional members of an average church who can really struggle with the idea that church is designed to be a place of intimacy and care. As you read, try to recognise yourself in this group before you start recognising others!

## Stoic Sam

There are people like Sam in every church—people who are rather against this new obsession with "airing your dirty laundry in public". Sam longs for a return to the good old days when people did not talk about their lives but just got on with studying the Bible and singing hymns. It was simpler then. He finds all these stories and emotions very tiresome.

Sam grew up in a time and culture in which there was great hardship and great pressure to be strong. There was no one to turn to for help when life was hard, so you just put one foot in front of the other. He learned that you survive best if you keep quiet and press any emotions down. And such a posture cannot be unlearned overnight.

Sam's way of doing life is completely understandable given his background but very different from the deep openness we see in Scripture. All those psalms (many of them written by David, who certainly was a strong man) show us that biblical men (and women) are designed to be people with soft hearts, willing and able to show their pain and their delight. The laments of Jeremiah and the tears of Jesus continue to build a picture of the goodness of showing vulnerability and, where appropriate, of crying. If in doubt, spend a few hours reading the psalms and underline every moment of self-disclosure and every deeply emotional word you read—such things are there in abundance!

Sam means no harm. Indeed he probably thinks he is being gospel-hearted when he encourages people to spend less time talking about themselves and more time focusing on truth. But he actually ends up being a stumbling block to the church becoming what they are designed to be. It is fine if he does not want to tell everyone everything (no one needs to do that), but by saying nothing to anyone about how he is really doing, he is in effect disconnecting himself from the community who are called to weep and rejoice together. He is depriving himself of the love and care that is rightfully his. He is depriving others of the privilege of sharing life with him and serving him. Indeed, others might even be scared to share when he is around.

I have few memories of my maternal grandfather—he died when I was very young—but one thing I do remember is his wooden leg. (Back in those days, it really was wooden.) To me, it appeared that sometimes he had a leg, and sometimes he didn't. Sam is the relational equivalent of a wooden leg: sometimes he is joined to the daily life of the church; sometimes he is separated. And that is not how any part of the body should be. We need to want better for Sam rather than to leave him to it—to love him enough to help him move away from stoicism towards Christ. That may be a slow journey and a hard one, but it will be one that will help the whole church grow.

## Fearful Fernanda

Fernanda's story is one of pain too. Unlike Sam, who keeps himself to himself because he thinks it is right to do so, Fernanda keeps her life locked away because she is terrified she will be hurt again. And who can blame her? If someone has been hurt deeply, they do not want to repeat the experience. But, like Sam, Fernanda is partially disconnected from those around her because her walls are so high.

It is worth stating clearly that while God calls churches to be places where lives are shared—as Paul modelled with the Thessalonians (1 Thessalonians 2:8)—churches are never places of forced sharing. We do not drag the details of people's lives out of them against their will. To do so would be horribly controlling. I have known the sadness of walking alongside people who have escaped from cults where they were expected to share thoughts, confess sins and divulge dreams in ways that left them more like the prey of their religious communities than precious members. We meet people where they are and show them, with abundant evidence, that we can be trusted—and we exercise consistent tenderness and patience as they begin to explore what trusting us might look like.

Here, too, the journey may be slow. Fernanda may never get to the place where she wants to share deeply, but, with enough love and reassurance, she can begin to trust again—and when she does, it will be a truly beautiful thing.

## Legalistic Laurence

Human beings do not fit into nice, neat boxes. In many situations, there is not one right choice and one wrong choice. Life is rather more complex than that! But people like Laurence do not like that complexity; they want clarity at every turn. Laurence simply seems to be naturally wired for right and wrong. In any given situation, he just wants to know what he should do—and he wants to be able to tell others the same.

Truth be told, sometimes Laurence's gift of clarity can be a joy. When a member of the congregation said he was being tempted to watch porn, Laurence was able to reel off a catalogue of biblical reasons why that was not going to be a good idea. His encyclopaedic knowledge effortlessly recalled every verse about purity. Everyone smiled, including the man who had shared his temptation. "Well, that's a fairly convincing list!" he replied. Of course, that was not the only thing the man needed to hear in his struggles, but Laurence's razor-sharp clarity had its role.

Things did not go so well when a woman in the congregation opened up about the deep pain she was experiencing at home. After a while, she said she was considering leaving her husband. "Divorce is wrong," said Laurence. "You need to repent of considering that." She had not mentioned divorce; he simply assumed that that was where "leaving" would lead. His response was based on a few verses of the Bible that he thought made things clear, rather than a fuller engagement with Scripture that would have produced a more nuanced approach. He had not wrestled with the concept of justice. He had not thought about the risks she was facing. He did not like conversations where lots of factors had to be taken into account. Unsurprisingly, the woman in question did not want to speak again in a group containing Laurence.

Laurence has many strengths but he, and those of us like

him, need to wrestle with the fact that life is rarely straightforward. That takes Laurence out of his comfort zone—it nudges him to have to think in ways that do not seem natural at all. He may need help to check out his pastoral responses before he utters them. He may need help to remember that grace is our driver, not law.

## Overcommitted Olivia

Olivia is a delight. She is one of the most loving and caring people you could meet—she is totally on board with the concept of a church that cares. But she is exhausted. What with work and home life and looking after elderly parents and the trusteeship of a local charity as well as church responsibilities, her diary is rammed. She is known to be wonderfully wise, but most people do not contact her. Why? Because they know she does not have time. Deep down, she knows it too. If she were to add another plate to the number she already has spinning, it is likely they would all come crashing to the ground. And yet she keeps saying yes to things.

There are often a lot of Olivias in the local church. There is something about the evangelical church that can breed overcommitment and even a prizing of doing too many things. Olivia simply does not have the time to share her life and love others well. It is not as simple as asking Olivia to slow down. She lost the brakes of her life many years ago, and she cannot just give up the many things she loves or currently needs to do—but we can help her grow. We can help Olivia look at her heart and see what is motivating her to push herself so hard. We can accompany her on one of her errands and chat in the car about who she is loving, what she is fearing, what she is seeking, who she is trying to please as she rushes around doing many things. Little by little, her diary may ease. Over time, she may begin to see the wonder that it is to just spend time with God and with her friends, not achieving but just being. And as she grows in these ways, she will help the rest of her church to flourish in their calling.

### Surface-level Saj

Saj is the kind of guy who always has a verse to share. He loves God's word. He knows God speaks through it today. He is gloriously confident that the Bible is powerful and good. And he wants to be part of the process of encouraging others in the local church with God's word.

His instincts are great, but the delivery sometimes leaves a lot to be desired. He plays a sort of "spiritual snap". You may remember the childhood card game—see an ace, place another ace on top of it and shout "snap", and you've made your match and won your cards. He does that with people's lives. You're anxious? Do not be anxious about anything! You're sad? Why are you downcast! You're grieving? Do not grieve without hope. It is as if he hears a key word in a sentence—such as anxiety, grief, or sadness—and then finds a verse with that word in it… snap!

The trouble is that Saj never takes the time to really listen to what is going on in someone's life. He sees a problem and seeks to find a verse to fix it. It does not occur to him that there might be many layers of hurt beneath the short sentence that someone has uttered and that a completely different place in Scripture might be the best place to go to. He comes across as simplistic—as someone who tries to put a biblical sticking plaster on even the most gaping of wounds and then thinks that that's a job well done. He is slightly feared in the church WhatsApp groups he is in. When someone shares their pain, he's a little too quick to offer that brilliant verse that's going to make everything right. He is reluctant to ask people questions that go deeper. He does not have much time for mess, questions or lament.

There is so much to encourage in Saj's life—if only we all had his passion for God's word! But little by little, there are areas where we may need to help him grow. If he doesn't, people will become more reluctant to share their lives with him. Helping him see the depths, the complexity of people's lives and the ways in which Scripture gives voice to confusion, pain and grief without having to rush to a solution will be an important first step.

## Evangelistic Eve

Eve is the kind of person most churches would like in their congregation. She is so passionate to share the gospel with those who do not yet know Christ. She will talk to anyone about Jesus; even taking delivery of a takeaway or Amazon package is fertile ground for a conversation about the Lord she loves so much. She has walked alongside many who have come to Christ—her ability with conversational apologetics is wonderful. However, she is so passionate about proclaiming Christ that she does not have much sympathy with Christians who are struggling in the day to day. Eternity is what matters to her and not so much the here and now. She has been known to mutter that pastoral care is too inward-looking when people need to be reaching out.

It is easy to see Eve's gifts and strengths. The church would be in a much healthier place if more of us would embody that call to hold out words of life to those who need to hear. But her weaknesses are on view too. Her contention that evangelism looks out and pastoral care looks in is just wrong. Both look up to Christ—both point people to the one they need most. As we saw in chapter 1, pastoral care can commend the gospel to those who do not yet know its wonder. And Scripture is clear that making disciples is not just about helping people move from death to life—it's about walking alongside people day by day until Jesus calls them home, knowing that we need each other if we are truly to live for Christ and honour him in all we do.

Eve might be the kind of person who, when it comes to church budgets, nudges the church leadership to spend on mission rather than pastoral care. Her stance might grow a culture in the church that the "better" Christians do evangelism while the "lesser" Christians stay behind and care. But Jesus cares for the whole person, across the whole of time. And helping Eve wrestle with that—maybe through the early chapters of Acts or indeed the earthly ministry of Christ—may be an important step to helping the church grow.

## Affirming Adele

Everyone likes Adele. She is so sympathetic and kind. Always willing to lend an ear, she is known to listen well to people's pain. And, after she has listened, she is wonderfully quick to affirm. Her words overflow with reminders that her friends are loved, forgiven and delighted in by the Lord. You cannot have a conversation with Adele and fail to be encouraged!

However, some topics of conversation are noticeable by their absence when you talk with Adele. She never talks about sin, never encourages confession, and never talks about the need to change. If you were to ask her directly, she would say we are all sinners in need of a Saviour, but she cannot bring herself to talk about that with friends. She fears that people might not like it—that it might cause disagreement. She wants all her conversations to feel nice.

What we don't want for Adele is for her to become harsh and a sin-hunter. Her gentleness is a joy—and often, when talking with people who feel broken, there is wisdom in not talking about sin too quickly. But sometimes the path to hope and freedom involves talking about hard things. Minimising or ignoring someone's sin may actually keep them trapped. Adele may be the kind of person to whom we want to say, "How can you use your beautiful gentleness and patience to help people see where their heart is going astray?"

## Not-me Norman

Finally, there are those who dwell on the edge of the church—people who love to receive care from the church leadership when life is hard but for whom the idea of being involved in caring for others seems a million miles away. Norman attends church more than he is actively involved in it. He is like a spectator at a football match, happy to watch the players run around doing Christian things (at least as long as things are going the way he wants) but with no interest in getting on the pitch and becoming involved in the game. Let those who are paid to care do the caring, he says.

Norman grew up in a church tradition where leaders did indeed do everything. Congregation members turned up, watched and said amen. He has always believed that if you are paying someone to do a job, then they should do it well, and you should not do it for them—and that is how he views his staff team.

Norman may or may not have a living faith. If he does not, there is no call for him to undertake the responsibilities of being part of a church. But if he does, then Norman is the kind of person with whom we may need to spend some quality time. There is a lot of unlearning of an unhelpful tradition to do—a lot of coming to see the church as it should be rather than as he has experienced it to be. It will be a slow process, but helping Norman see the beauty of serving together will be a wonderful thing.

Every church has a Sam, Fernanda, Laurence, Olivia, Saj, Norman, Adele and Eve. Most churches have considerably more than one. Indeed, it is highly likely that you can see elements of your own approach to church life that mesh with some of the characters mentioned here.

I do not mention such tendencies to induce guilt. The aim here is not to read these stories and think, "Oh, I am such an Olivia—what a miserable worm am I" but rather to acknowledge that there are barriers to a church becoming a place of care, and to acknowledge that some of those barriers are in our own heart. The good news, however, is that God is at work in all of our hearts. We are not going to stay the same. As we seek to follow Christ, we are growing to be more like Christ, and as we pursue the attitudes that God says are best, then every Sam, Fernanda, Laurence, Olivia, Saj, Norman and Eve can play a part in growing their church's culture into something more healthy—something that pleases the Lord who has saved them.

## Next steps

With the principles from the last three chapters in our minds, we are going to turn now to the practicalities of growing a culture of care. In other words, if we really do have this wonderful call, and if we really will face these real and difficult barriers, how do we actually move forward? In the chapters that follow, we will look at a range of areas that need addressing in order to promote a culture of care. As you read, you will find some things for you to do and some things to pray that others in your church will do. Churches are communities where the different parts work together, not solo pursuits. To that end, it might be a good idea to read this book with others in your church so you can think collectively about how to build this kind of culture. As you read, good questions to ask yourself are "What is my role and responsibility in this area? And what would it be good for me to discuss with someone else?"

## Questions for reflection

1. Out of all the characters in this chapter, who are you most like? Why do you think you have developed these traits?
2. How do you feel about the possibility of change—for the glory of God, for the good of the church and for the flourishing of yourself?
3. How are you going to pray for your own heart in light of what you have discovered today?

SECTION 2

# PRACTICALITIES OF CARING WELL

# CHAPTER 4

# DEPENDENCY: GROWING THROUGH PRAYER

If we are truly committed to being a church that loves others well, there is only one place to start: and that is on our knees. You cannot change your own heart; you cannot change other people's hearts; you cannot change your church. All of us are utterly reliant on God for such things, so talking to him about them is an absolute necessity and makes absolute sense.

"Yes, yes, prayer is obviously important," I hear you say. You know that, and I know that, but it so easily slips off the agenda. We often want to say a quick prayer and then skip on to the bit where we get to do things: the activity, the structure, the making things happen. For most of us, that's where our passion lies. It is not where the power lies though—that is with our heavenly King. So, we are going to take a slow walk through the importance of praying for our church because, if we really want to see them grow in their love and care, this is how it begins.

## Spend time with the one you want to be like

Have you ever noticed how you become like the people you spend time with? Some of us might display this tendency more than others, but we all do it to a certain extent. We pick up some of the vocabulary that the people around us use. We imbibe some of the values that they espouse. Sometimes we begin to dress like them or watch the same shows as them. The way we live is a little bit contagious.

Maybe we see that most noticeably in families. It is a constant source of amusement to me how much I am becoming like my mother. All those little things she used to say and do (all those things that used to irritate me endlessly) can now be seen in me. I've become like her. We see that tendency in the church too—we assimilate into the community. That is probably why the wisdom literature of the Old Testament is so keen to remind us that who we spend time with matters. The righteous choose their friends carefully (Proverbs 12:26).

There is an even more important component to this though. We become like God when we spend time with him—not primarily when we do things for him but when we sit and spend quality time focusing on him, enjoying his presence. We do that partly as we hear from him in his word, and we do it partly as we talk to him in prayer. That is how relationships grow: through time spent listening and speaking with one another. That is why Jesus commended Mary, who sat at his feet, more than Martha, who was scurrying around being very busy (Luke 10:42).

If you are someone who is very active, passionate and driven (a bit like me), you might find this hard—not all of us are naturally wired for slow conversation. But it is so important. We do not become like the people with whom we exchange a few text messages here and there, and we do not become like God when we throw the odd arrow prayer in his direction and get on with our to-do list.

So what might it look like to spend quality time with him? It will not come by resolving to do our "quiet times" and then treating them as something on our to-do list. Relationship-building is not an action point. Rather, it looks like choosing to spend time with our heavenly Father just because he loves us and we love him in return. So...

- Try picking up your Bible, finding a comfy chair, reading a passage and then talking to God about what excites you, confuses you, challenges you and/or encourages you. Studying in a more structured way absolutely has its place, but sometimes it is good simply to curl up with God's word and read it as you would read a tender letter from your favourite relative or friend, and respond in the same natural way.
- Try going for a walk somewhere beautiful—a park, a canal bank, some rolling fields—and chat to God about what you see. Thank him for the beautiful things (notice just how many wonderful things there are) and praise him for the intricacy and diversity you can see and the way the world all holds together. Ask him to be at work in the things that are not as they should be.
- Pick an attribute of God—for instance his holiness, his gentleness, his strength or his presence—and talk to him about what that means. You might find it helpful to meditate on a verse of Scripture to fuel your thinking, but tell him what you love about that attribute, and anything you find hard too.
- Draw a picture (or find one online) of one of the ways God is described in the Bible (rock, refuge, stronghold, shepherd, king, light, bread... there are so many!). Talk to him about how that particular activity or image makes a difference to you and your church. Ask for his help to grasp it more and more.

You can be as creative as you like in terms of methodology. The idea is to engage with God in ways that are faithful and deeply relational. Enjoy time with God and see how that begins to change the way you view him, speak to him and trust him.

## Spend time acknowledging your utter dependence

It is an incredible privilege to be able to speak to God in a relaxed and familial way. Such a privilege came at a high price—Jesus' life—but it is one we can revel in. However, we do need to be careful to remember his greatness too. He is closer than a brother, but he's not simply a good mate with a lot of power. God is God, and one thing we absolutely need to grasp is how small we are compared with him.

This can be a struggle. Often Christians run to one extreme or the other. At one pole we might think, "I am small. I'm nothing. I don't matter at all." That is not what the Bible says. We are all made in God's image (Genesis 1:26-27), knitted together by him in our mother's womb (Psalm 139:13). Those in Christ are chosen and are called "children of God", bought at a price and loved beyond measure (Ephesians 1:3-14). Being small does not mean being a waste of space. On the other hand, at the other pole we find people reacting very strongly, stamping their feet and demanding acknowledgement that they are strong and important, and even pivotal to God's plan. Apologies for the slightly blunt raincheck, but there is nothing pivotal about any of us. We are weak and dependent. And that is okay.

Being weak and dependent is exactly how we are designed to be. He is the Creator; we are his creations. He is the Saviour; we are the saved. He is the Shepherd; we are the sheep. He is the Potter; we are the clay. God's power is made perfect in our weakness (2 Corinthians 12:9). Getting that straight in our heads does not mean we have to go about feeling bad about ourselves or beating ourselves up. It means rejoicing in the fact that he is so much bigger and better than us and then enjoying the fact that we get to know him and join in with his eternal plans.

As our hearts fill with awe and wonder at who God is and as we see that we can do nothing without him, we will become ever more like the builder who built his home on solid rock and less like the builder who built his home on the sand (Matthew 7:24-27). What might that look like? When it comes to becoming a congregation that cares, it means starting with humility—starting by saying, "Lord, I can't do this; we can't do this, no matter how hard we try. Lord, come and do this work in us—build your church and make us more like you. Help me listen to you, lean on you, trust you and follow you in every aspect of this process. I need you."

## Spend time praying for your church

One of the clearest signs that we are becoming like Jesus and leaning on Jesus is that we grow in our eagerness to pray for the things that matter to Jesus. And the church matters to Jesus so much. He is the foundation—the head. He calls his people into the church. He will preserve us for eternity. He cares whether your church—every church—is becoming the loving community they are designed to be.

- We can talk to him about the growth of care within our church.
- We can ask him to help us see him and hear his call more clearly.
- We can ask him to help us follow him into an increasingly loving future.
- We can ask him to work in the hearts of those who are finding the idea hard.
- We can ask him to forgive us when we say unloving things or act in unloving ways.
- We can ask him to build a sense of unity within the church as the calling is pursued.

The list can go on. Why not jot down a few ideas of what you might pray for your church now?

Some wonderful places in which to begin are the prayers of Paul. Ephesians 3 contains this prayer:

> *"And I pray that you, being rooted and established in love, may have power, together with all the Lord's holy people, to grasp how wide and long and high and deep is the love of Christ, and to know this love that surpasses knowledge—that you may be filled to the measure of all the fullness of God." (v 17-19)*

You can pray through this a couple of verses at a time, confident that you are praying something that is close to God's heart. Have a go at rooting each clause in a real situation or the real people in your church. God loves to say yes to prayers like these.

The reality is, however, that often we get quite excited about praying for our church for a season and then… we stop. Maybe after reading a book (or chapter!) that encourages us to pray, we set out with good intentions, but after a while, other things crowd in, and we forget. Or maybe we have been praying for a while, and nothing much seems to be happening, so we get disillusioned. This is where we need one another. A church that grows together is a church that prays together.

If you are a church leader, can you make praying for the church to grow in their love and care for one another a regular item in elders' meetings, Sunday services and midweek prayer meetings? If you are someone that leads prayers during services, you can regularly include church growth in this area as a recurring point in your prayers. If you are in a midweek group, maybe you can suggest this becomes a prayer item each time you meet. If you are someone who is just passionate about praying for this, why not grab a friend and undertake to call each other for ten minutes a week/fortnight/month and pray together on the phone. We are all so much more likely to keep praying if we do so together. Praying that the Lord will help the church flourish can be a unifying, encouraging, and emboldening activity.

### Spend time praying for yourself

Along the way, it is wise to pray for ourselves. As we embark on this exciting journey of helping our churches become places of deeper love and care, we might find all kinds of desires rising in our hearts.

Maybe there will be impatience; we want our church to be more loving, and we want them to be more loving now. Churches grow slowly, and a willingness to move at the pace the congregation can cope with will be necessary.

Maybe there will be frustration at things that have been less than ideal. It is important that we do not let frustration seep into our prayers. "Lord, this week please let us love each other better than we did last Wednesday" is not going to be a helpful phrase to say out loud. Asking the Lord for the strength to bear with those who are tripping up is key.

Maybe there is one person in the congregation who seems to be opposing the change you would like to see. For some reason, they just are not heading or responding to the call. It will be easy to view them as a problem, not a precious image-bearer—to see their resistance as something that defines them rather than a facet of them. Asking for the Lord's help to love them will be an act of deep humility and trust.

Maybe there has been deep pain in the past for you. I don't mean just sinful people being sinful but a huge hurt that you've suffered in the context of church. The pain of such experiences is not to be underestimated. It can leave us reeling, feeling angry and afraid. Such things are often best processed alongside a wise friend or counsellor, but prayer is crucial too. Ask the Lord to bind up your broken heart to enable you to recapture the beauty of what the church is designed to be, to uphold justice on your behalf, and to help you learn to trust again.

We are human. Some ungodly thoughts will cross our minds. There will be moments when we will need to repent of our prayerlessness or the pointed prayers we have prayed. There will probably be times when we need to repent of avoiding certain people or pressuring those people who do not seem to understand how beautiful it is to pursue being a church that offers Christ-like care. There is grace in abundance for times like these. God's desire to forgive those who turn to him in faith does not run out.

But lastly, we can also pray prayers of praise for what God has done in us. How wonderful it is when we see our hearts softening to those around us. How glorious it is when the fruit of the Spirit flourishes more in our lives (Galatians 5:22-23). What a work of grace it is when we become quicker to repent of the ungodly attitudes that linger in our hearts. What a reason to praise it is when we see God's work in us and begin to realise that if he can do that in us, he can do that in every member of our church.

Weak is how we are designed to be. Embracing that is utterly liberating. And it will lead us to pray with a passion—and, as we pray to the God who can do more than we can ask for or even imagine (Ephesians 3:20), we and those around us will begin to change.

## Questions for reflection

1. What is getting in the way of you spending quality time with the Lord? How can you address this?
2. What can you pray now for your church?
3. What can you pray now for yourself?

CHAPTER 5

# COMMUNITY: GROWING THROUGH RELATIONSHIPS

Relationships matter in the body of Christ. What we share, how we share it, how we respond to others and what our posture is towards our brothers and sisters in Christ all build together to produce a culture that can be gloriously encouraging, disappointingly superficial, or deeply disturbing.

We know this from our own experience. If we share some wonderful news, we want those around us to share our joy—and if they don't, we feel somewhat deflated. If we share something hard, we want those around us to acknowledge our pain—if they don't, we feel misunderstood and unloved. Appropriate intimacy brings community, and distance breeds isolation; but being attentive to relationships can seem hard at times. In the busyness of church life, it can be tempting simply to focus on the things that need to be done. There are the Bible-study questions that need writing, the coffee that needs making, the talk that needs preparing, the clearing up of Bibles and stacking of chairs that has to be done before the doors are locked. These all vie for our attention and scream, "Let's be as efficient as we can be". Relationships are not efficient. They do not have a concrete end point that allows you to say, "That's all done". They are, however, a biblical priority in a local church—something that is essential if we are to love and care well. This is something the apostle Paul knew very well.

## The priority of relationships

When Paul visited the Greek city of Thessalonica, he did not have an easy time. He had recently faced significant opposition in Philippi, which had left him and his companions battered and bruised (Acts 16). Once in Thessalonica, things did not improve. His preaching started a riot, and he ended up having to face the city officials again (17:1-9). Amid such pressures, it might be understandable if Paul were to become very insular—yes, continuing to preach the gospel but other than that, spending time with just a small group of trusted gospel workers and not worrying about the softer skills of relationship-building. We might also tend to think that a man so determined to share Christ with the Gentiles could get quite driven and single-minded about gospel proclamation at the expense of all else.

Yet that is not what happened.

Paul did preach the gospel fearlessly and clearly in Thessalonica. He was not deterred from continuing his itinerant mission work (next stop Berea). His passion for evangelism was absolutely clear. And yet he describes his time with the Thessalonians like this:

> *"We were gentle among you, like a nursing mother caring for her children. We cared so deeply that we were delighted to share with you not only the gospel of God, but our own lives as well. That is how beloved you have become to us."*
>
> *(1 Thessalonians 2:7-8, Majority Standard Bible)*

When the pressure was on, Paul chose gentleness in relationships. When the stakes were high, he prioritised nurturing those around him. When opposed, he cared deeply for others. When his liberty was at risk, he nevertheless was delighted to share his life with others in the church. Though he knew his stay was temporary, he sought to get to know the brothers and sisters so well that he could describe them as his beloved. In the middle of the urgency of gospel proclamation and the danger of physical persecution, Paul prioritised deep relationships with the church. He loved them, and they loved him in return. It is worth asking ourselves the question: in our more comfortable circumstances, are we willing to do the same?

## The pursuit of relationships

One of the reasons why Paul prioritised relationships is because he saw other people through the lens of Christ. Jesus—God come down—had every right to claim authority. He had every right to be unknowable. He had every right to keep his distance. God does not have to share his space with messy, sinful, ridiculously unwise human beings. Yet he did. That is exactly what Jesus chose to do throughout his earthly ministry.

Jesus called an unlikely rag-tag bunch of disciples, many of whom had some fairly substantial spiritual heart defects, and spent three years sharing his life with them. Matthew (with his background in dishonest tax affairs), Peter (with his serious impulse-control problems), Thomas (with a notable wobbliness in his faith) and Judas (who could not keep his hands out of the petty cash) became his close friends. They ate with him, walked with him, listened to him, met members of his family and introduced members of their family to him. They watched him, learned to imitate him, prayed with him and even saw him die. With the notable exception of Judas, they got to know him so well that they were able to tell others about him in extraordinary detail and even to write biographies of him with an authority and accuracy that could withstand the Roman rumour-machine that wanted to paint Jesus in a very different light. Within the band of twelve were the three (Peter, James and John) who became especially close to Jesus, joining him on some of the more intimate ministry excursions. Beyond the band of twelve were the 70: other followers who got to know Jesus slightly less well. Those included people from all walks of life, including women working on the streets and those with diseases that caused most people to steer clear. Jesus, in the most pressured of circumstances (pressure does not come any bigger than a mission to save the world) consistently pursued and prioritised relationships.

No wonder, then, that Jesus' followers are called to be people who pursue relationships too. We absolutely have a clear and exciting call to spread the gospel—the Great Commission of Matthew 28 makes that clear—but not at the expense of relationships. We are called to move towards people and spend time with them. These people we are to move towards include those who are like us and those who are not—and we're not just to let them see a glimpse of our lives but also for instance, to eat together regularly as the early church did (Acts 2:46) and open our homes as Lydia did (16:15).

## The intimacy of relationships

Christ-centred relationships are designed to be close ones. As we can see from the life of Jesus, there are different levels of closeness. Peter, James and John were Jesus' closest friends. The other nine disciples were close but knew him slightly less. The 70 were a little more distant but still pretty close to the centre. After Judas' betrayal, his replacement, Matthias, was chosen from this group (Acts 1:26). Not everyone is equally close, but closeness in general is meant to be the norm in a believing community.

We see this kind of dynamic with Paul too. He had some particularly close friends—people like Silas and Timothy, with whom he did so much of his travelling—but there was also a level of intimacy with the other disciples, with the elders of the churches he planted and with the congregations too. He genuinely shared not just the gospel but his life with them. That is why he could write to them with such intimacy, even naming people he was particularly appreciative of or worried about. That is why he could express his need openly in his letters (see, for example, 2 Timothy 4:13, 16).

What might this sharing of lives, this intimacy, look like for us? It will mean having some friendships in the church within which we are pretty comprehensively known. It is never possible to know a person fully, but we can all have friends whom we let into our hearts and lives in significant ways. Friends like that will know what makes us laugh and what makes us cry. They will be aware of the good things and the hard things in our life. They will know how our faith is doing. They will be aware of where our heart is leaning towards rebellion. They will be able to observe how we are growing. They will be able to spot where we are persevering. And they will know all that not because we have been forced to share the information but because it is a mutual joy to share life with one another. They will know us so well that they can pray for us with special wisdom and speak to us with extraordinary insight. They will feel our delights and our pain.

We will also have other relationships in which we see some of what has just been described above but not all of it. These will be people who have a general sense of how we are doing—enough to be able to pray for and encourage us well. They will know the big things in our life but not all the detail.

And then we will have relationships that are honest but more distant—people who know us enough to be able to enjoy the good and pray in general ways for things that are hard.

Such relationships do not appear overnight. They take a while to develop. Everyone we meet starts on the outer ring of our friendships and it is over time—as experiences are shared, as we come together round God's word, as we pray together, as we discover that others are trustworthy—that we begin to share a little more. Gradually, intimacy can grow. Gradually, we work out who will be a good choice for our closest friends. Gradually, acquaintances become friends.

The call is, within our church, to have a tendency towards sharing in all relationships but a wisdom that acknowledges that telling everyone everything is never wise.

## The wisdom of relationship

Like the three bears in the story of Goldilocks, some of us can be too hot or too cold when it comes to sharing. There are those who tend to want to share with everyone—stories of pain tumble out and the most intimate details are revealed in a first conversation. That is too hot. That kind of relationship forgets that not everyone can hold the position of knowing the details. Relationships have to grow; they cannot spontaneously appear. It may take years for two people to be ready to give and receive the intimacy of being a close friend.

Then there are those who want to share nothing. That is too cold. An individual, can never flourish as an island. When we have been hurt in the past, it is completely understandable that we may be reticent about opening up again, and certainly there should be no pressure to go deep quickly, but to be human is to share lives. In Genesis 1 and 2, Adam and Eve walked in the garden and had no secrets from each other or God. That is what we were created for. In this fallen world, we do need to exercise more caution than the first humans did in the perfection of the newly created world, but our posture—our nature—is to be known.

To continue the Goldilocks analogy, what does "just right" look like? It would be unwise to be too prescriptive. Your personal history, your culture and your church setting will all impact what is possible and what is best. Maybe wisdom would say that "just right" simply looks like being a believer who has a desire to grow their relationships ever deeper: not recklessly running towards destructive relationships but carefully pursuing Christ-honouring ones, where sharing lives is beautiful and enables a mutual flourishing in the faith.

When we each do this, the culture of our church begins to change and grow.

## Some relationship FAQs

In a book of this length, we cannot cover every eventuality, but before we conclude this chapter on relationships and sharing lives, it is worth addressing a few common questions.

1. *When you talk about feeling each other's joy and pain, are you talking about empathy? Some people would say that empathy is a sin.*
   Empathy has become an unexpectedly controversial term in recent years. Some say that identifying closely with a person will always end up with us affirming them—even affirming their sin—and that is unhelpful, ungodly and just plain wrong. Empathy is indeed the act of identifying with another person closely—being so in sync with them that you feel their joy and their pain—but not in a way that automatically affirms. In identifying closely with another person, we come to understand them in profound ways and, as such, are able to respond to them wisely. Empathy, when rightly understood, models Romans 12:15

and liberates us to weep with those who weep and rejoice with those who rejoice. It is a unifying act, but it is never an act that causes us to leave our brain or Bible at the door. We can weep with a man who is grieving, identifying with his pain, but that does not mean affirming the cruel words he speaks in his grief. Empathy does not mean we unquestioningly affirm, but it does mean we understand someone profoundly both on an intellectual and emotional level and love them deeply by being with them in their pain before we speak to them in whatever ways God would call us to respond.

2. *Are you suggesting I prioritise church relationships over non-Christian friends?*
   We all need a range of friends. While we are not of the world, God does call us to be in the world (John 17:16, 18) and that means we will want to spend quality time with people outside God's kingdom as well as those who are inside. We will be keen to share the gospel with our neighbours, and that will involve loving them well. If we have non-Christian family, there will be a particular need to spend time with them, honouring them as God would have us do. Nonetheless, our relationships within church are designed to have a different quality to relationships outside the church—speaking the truth in love with one another is the calling of the church community, and it is good to invest in doing that well.

3. *I work for the church. Can I have friends in the church?*
   Being a church leader is a complex role. People often relate to pastors and other gospel workers (and their spouses) slightly differently, and that can make

friendship hard. However, pastors and other staff members do need friends, and to say that relationships within the church matter for everyone other than those paid to serve there would be very odd. There is no sense that the early apostles distanced themselves from relationships within the church (even though they clearly also had deep friendships with others in ministry). There is nothing in Scripture that would suggest that the biblical injunction to share lives does not apply to church leaders. There may be some things that church leaders choose to share with others in church leadership elsewhere rather than with their congregation members but, overall, welcoming pastors as friends and encouraging them to develop some close friendships within the church is biblical, wise and good for the whole church. (That said, remembering church leaders cannot be close friends with everyone is also important.)

4. *What if I've been really hurt by sharing my life and I don't want to go there again?*
   Being hurt at church is devastating. You will no doubt need time to rest, recover and process what you have been through. There is no pressure to rush into sharing again. Depending on what happened, there may be a case for seeking justice or calling out the behaviour that hurt you so badly, and counselling may be useful to help you process your pain and enable you to start the long journey towards forgiveness. However, sharing life is what you are designed for, and eventually moving in that direction again will help you flourish. Take your time but prepare your heart, and please do not let the pain of the past deprive you of the joy and fullness of intimacy in the future.

5. *I'm a woman. Should I seek to be good friends with a man? (And vice versa.)*
The Bible tells us that our relationships within the church are primarily those of brothers and sisters, and in healthy families brothers and sisters can spend quality time together without there being any problems. Jesus, as the perfect man, modelled having close relationships with women like Mary and Martha, and also had no problem having an in-depth conversation with the woman at the well (John 4—this would have been shocking given the cultural norms of the day). The biblical call to share lives, then, is not just a call to share lives with people of the same gender. However, there is also biblical warrant for particularly deep relationships—such as mentoring relationships—being conducted by women with women and men with men (Titus 2:1-8). This, then, is an area where we need wisdom: there is no biblical call for men and women to avoid each other, treat each other with suspicion or pull back from talking together, but we are to act in ways that are above reproach, making sure that both men and women avoid leading each other into temptation in the area of sexual sin. Maybe the best way to do this is to ensure that friendships between men and women are known about rather than hidden—it is always in the darkness that sin thrives, not the light.

6. *What if there is a culture of gossip in my church?*
Gossip is dangerous. The Bible calls those who gossip fools (Proverbs 10:18) and is clear that gossip leads to broken relationships (Proverbs 16:28) and usually leads to increasing ungodliness (2 Timothy 2:16). Sharing the details of your life with someone who gossips is deeply unwise. If the church is a place of gossip,

that is something that needs addressing both through teaching from the front and through godly individuals being willing to say, with humility, "This conversation is not honouring Jesus; let's stop". Gradually culture can change, but it is certainly fair to only share limited areas of your life while the culture persists.

7. *Should I only share with people who are completely safe?* Sadly, there is no such thing as a fully safe person—not this side of heaven. To be in a relationship is to take risks. The risk is usually worth it—relationships are beautiful, and imperfections often help us grow! Having said that, there is no biblical call to share lives with abusive, coercive or manipulative people. It is not wise to give a controlling person ammunition with which to hurt you. It is wise to move towards a fallible person, though, and enjoy growing your Christ-centred relationship together through the ups and downs which that will bring. That is what a church truly is.

## Questions for reflection

1. With whom are you able to share your life in intimate ways? Praise God for those people now.
2. How would you like your relationships to grow? What areas of your life might you helpfully share with close friends? Who might you pray for—that you and they might become closer?
3. Are there any unwise relational dynamics in your life that you need to repent of? Are there any unwise relational dynamics in the church that need prayer—and possibly someone addressing them directly? Are you the person to say something, or would it be best to liaise with someone in the church who is better placed to do so?

# CHAPTER 6

# ATTENTIVENESS: GROWING THROUGH LISTENING

So far we have looked at two foundational pieces of growing a culture of care in the local church. We have seen that prayer is essential and that a desire to know and be known is vital. Without the Lord's work and a commitment to increasingly shared lives, everything else we do will be hollow. However, if those things are in place, then there is much we can do to help a culture of care flourish. The first of those is to listen well to the people around us.

## Listen up

It is so irritating when people do not listen. I remember being in a season when I was quite tired. The person I was speaking with told me to book a holiday, stop finding my identity in my work and read my Bible more. On the surface, maybe those don't seem like strange things to say. After all, we have a biblical mandate to rest, my identity should be in Christ, not in my work, and engaging with Scripture is of primary importance. The problem was that those comments were made without the other person listening to me, and, as such, they completely missed the mark. I already had a holiday in the diary, but it had been thwarted by a close family member ending up in hospital fighting for their life. I absolutely do have idols in my heart, but that was not driving my exhaustion at that time—sitting in ITU was. And my lack of Bible reading had nothing to do with spiritual drought and everything to do with the tears in my eyes making reading hard. Safe to say, those theologically accurate comments fell on me like a ton of bricks and provided absolutely no help whatsoever. The conversation ended without that person ever knowing that I had a relative who was seriously ill, because they never asked what was going on in my life or what was behind the bags under my eyes, and I struggled to get a word in. After a while, I didn't want to get a word in—I just wanted them to go away. If only they had listened!

That might be a slightly stark example, but there are plenty of others in most churches week by week. We miss what is really going on for our brothers and sisters in Christ because we do not take the time to really ask and to really hear how they are doing.

## Listen like God

Listening is an extremely God-like thing to do. God listens to us all the time. In fact, he loves to hear us and answer us (1 John 5:14). In Scripture, we see examples of God listening to prayer, to lament, to questions, to fears and to repentance—the Psalms are full of words sung to God. He welcomes our words because he is keen for us to build up our relationship with him and keen to respond.

We see that same attentiveness modelled by Jesus. When we think of his earthly ministry, we rightly give most of our attention to what he said and did, but he did not just teach—he asked people great questions, listened to the answers and then often asked something more.

The woman at the well in John 4 is a great case in point. Jesus starts the conversation by asking her a question: "Will you give me a drink?" (v 7). He listens to her answer and her confusion at his request (v 9) and responds with a tantalising statement to pique her interest in spiritual things (v 10). Later in the conversation, he asks about her husband and listens to her answer, and shows extraordinary knowledge of her situation (v 17-18). This leads on to her seeing Jesus more clearly (as a prophet) and being willing to engage in deeper spiritual conversation. She ends up discovering that he is the Messiah (v 25-26, 29).

Could Jesus have just told this woman to repent and believe? Yes, but he chose not to. He chose to ask, listen and engage with the person in front of him, and that bore wonderful fruit.

## Listen to God

If our churches are to flourish, we need to be multi-directional listeners. The first direction we need to be listening in is listening to God—listening to him in his word as the Spirit applies it to our hearts.

Everything we need to know about how to be church—how to worship God, how to love one another, how to prioritise relationships, how to share lives, how to encourage, spur on and challenge—is in Scripture. It is sufficient—every page of it is useful for equipping us to live lives that honour Christ (2 Timothy 3:16-17). It is our highest authority and our greatest joy. It is something we are called to meditate upon (Psalm 119:15) and obey (v 7). It is even something we are called to sing out (v 54) because God's word makes us wise and keeps us walking rightly with the Lord (v 104). That does not mean we never read any other books, but it does mean that nothing else defines and guides us as Scripture does. As God speaks, we are called to listen.

## Listen to one another

Listening has a strong horizontal component to it as well. When Paul, Peter, James and John first wrote their letters to the early church, they wanted the specific Christians in the specific churches to listen to their words. When they wrote their letters, they were responding to the specific needs in those churches—needs that they had ascertained by listening to the people there.

In Acts, we see people listening to each other and not just to the great sermons that were given. We see leaders listening to the complaints of the Greek widows when they were being overlooked in food distribution, and putting in place better ways of looking after those in need (Acts 6:1-6). We see church members listening to reports of the material needs of others and ensuring those needs were fulfilled (4:32-36). We see Paul listening to Lydia's desire to serve and accepting her invitation to stay in her home (16:15). We see Philip listening to the Ethiopian eunuch's confusion and answering his questions (8:26-39). Listening well is a crucial component of any church that wants to grow in love and service.

So how do we listen well?

## Listen without presuppositions

We can only listen well if we avoid making assumptions about people. The more we assume, the worse we will listen. Indeed, if we even begin to think that someone's problems are obvious or the solutions to their challenges clear, we will not listen, and we will misfire when we speak. No one's struggles are simple, and only rarely are the ways forward obvious. Life just is not like that. Complexity is much more likely, and to understand complexity, we will need to take the time to listen well. We can pray for ourselves, "Lord, help me to grasp how little I know, and then help me to understand what this person needs me to know".

## Listen with humility

The best starting point for listening is to acknowledge that you need help to understand another human being—help from God and help from the person in front of you.

Adopting a posture that says, "I am interested in you, and I want to know the real you" can be so helpful. Humility encourages a slow pace and understands that people may need time to share what is really going on. Humility encourages prayerfulness, asking the Lord that wisdom will be the lens through which the listening is done. Humility grows a desire to ask questions to clarify things that are unclear. We can pray for ourselves, "Lord, give me the patience and curiosity I need to know the person before me well. Help me not to be satisfied with phrases like, 'I'm fine' but to seek to serve the person before me in the situations they are facing."

### Listen with a desire to see the person flourish

There are many different motivations for listening. For instance, it is possible to listen to gain power, searching out information that can make us look good or be used against people. There is listening for entertainment, where we home in on things that bring us pleasure. We can listen for efficiency, focusing on the things we need to know in order to make a quick decision or progress a task; or for self-indulgence, as we revel in another person's misfortune or success. The call is to listen so we can get to know someone and, in whatever circumstances they are facing, point them to Jesus and walk with them the paths of faithfulness. If we want anything other than that they flourish in their faith and joy, our motives are impure. We can pray for ourselves, "Lord, let me want what you want for the person in front of me".

### Listen with good questions

Jesus was a master question-asker. As we listen, we can encourage people to share by asking good questions. The typical opening question, "How are you?" is likely to be met with the standard response, "Fine, thank you". Such an exchange is, well, fine as a greeting, but it rarely helps progress a conversation well. Questions like "What's encouraged you this week?" "What has been hard this week?" or "What's been hardest this week?" are more likely to be fertile ground. When you are with someone you know relatively well, you can go a little deeper: "What are you longing for in this season?" "What are you fearing?" "Where is the Lord in the middle of this situation?" Questions help someone unwrap their heart, one layer at a time. We need to be gentle with our questions—in a church we are people having a conversation rather than authorities engaging in an interrogation! And bear in mind that close friends can go deeper than new friends. Respect people when they choose not to answer—cults, not churches, demand that people share. But good questions, asked with humility and a desire to see people flourish, can help people feel known, seen, loved and heard.

### Listen to behaviour and emotions as well as words

Sometimes actions speak louder than words. When someone says they're fine but a tear is rolling down their cheek, it is likely that the tear is where the true story lies. When someone says they're happy but is stomping round the church stacking chairs in such a way that you fear for the very survival of each chair leg, it is the behaviour that tells the story that needs to be heard. If someone is angry but claiming to be calm, it may be unwise to draw attention to their anger there and then. But afterwards, once there has been a little space, follow up with questions like "I couldn't help noticing that you seemed to be displaying strong emotions while stacking those chairs—can I ask: what was going on for you then?" Exploring where words differ from actions or emotions can be fertile ground for getting to know someone well.

There are times when emotions will be very big indeed. It can be hard for people to open up about their struggles—tears or anger may flow. There may be times when it is difficult to see what is going on beneath the raw emotions, and those moments can be particularly confusing for the person listening. We may even be tempted to switch off or dismiss a conversation if we feel the person has become "too emotional". Those emotions are there for a reason though. In an initial conversation, all you might be able to do is hear the pain and pray for hope, and then later on you can explore more of what is going on underneath. It is worth holding gently the emotions of those you are speaking with and waiting for the right moment to ask more.

## Listen out for what is good, what is hard and what is ugly

As I listen, I find it useful to have a framework in mind. In any conversation, I may well be able to spot things that are of great encouragement—moments when the person talks about turning to the Lord, praising, repenting, persevering or changing. These are glorious moments of grace. How wonderful it is to be grace-hunters, people who are constantly on the lookout for where the Lord is at work and where people are growing to be more like Christ. Such things can be points on which we dwell—points where we encourage people with what we have seen. They can be moments when we stop, take stock and remind ourselves that God is active and good. Some of us are people who are difficult to encourage. We are only pleased when a sin has been conquered, suffering has ended, or a level of maturity has been reached. It is far better to be encouraged (and to share that encouragement) by every small step of growth and godliness we see.

Second, in any conversation I may well be able to spot things that are hard. Suffering, pain, injustice and trials may be burdening the life of the person I'm with. We live in a fallen world; we have done ever since Genesis 3, and every single human being has been impacted by the fall in multiple ways. I need to note the hard things, listen especially well to those hard things, and respond to them with compassion and care. If I do not see how hard someone is finding life, I may miss why they are finding it difficult to persevere or change. Applying appropriate gospel comfort and hope is a right response to seeing pain. Everyone benefits from hearing words of gentle tenderness from the Lord.

Third, I may be able to see things that are ugly—ways in which someone's heart is going deeply astray. There may be rebellion, hard-heartedness, and an entrenchment in sin. Some of us will be tempted to focus here at the expense of the other categories—our tendency will be to call people to repentance without acknowledging all the good and the hardship in their lives. If we take that approach, we will be cold and heartless friends. Others of us, however, will be tempted to avoid this ground, seeking to minimise sin: "Oh, we all do that—you're only human" or "I'm sure it wasn't that bad". Such a reluctance to see sin as it truly is keeps people trapped because it leads them away from the liberation and restoration that repentance brings. Being willing to see sin clearly, note its devastating effects, and yet have lips that drip with grace is wonderful. If we listen with that lens, as it were, we will be able to point people to hope that is extraordinary and complete.

Listening, of course, takes time. Remember, relationships are not efficient uses of time—they require investment that does not bring instant returns—but by listening we can get to know people well. And once we have got to know them, we are in a position to respond to them wisely and well, and they are in a position to know that they can trust us as we speak. This dynamic can help build any church.

## Questions for reflection

1. When have you known the pain of not being listened to? How would you have liked that person to listen to you?
2. How would you like to grow in this area of listening? Why not pray for that now?
3. What difference would it make to your church if everyone listened well to one another? Capture that vision and pray the Lord would bring it to pass.

CHAPTER 7

# GROWING THROUGH VISION-SETTING

So far, we have looked at what every individual member of the congregation can do to build a culture of love and care through prayer, posture, relationship-building and good listening. In this chapter, we are going to look at moving beyond what we can do on our own and thinking about how we can encourage others to come on board with the vision of a church that cares well.

A church is a body that is united. God made us that way when he called us together in Christ. It is never our job to create unity in the church, but it is our responsibility to maintain that unity (Ephesians 4:3). Part of that is going to mean helping people grasp the call to Christ-centred care and to join together in pursuing that calling.

## Concealing the vision

One of the best ways to ensure your congregation never grows in this area of caring for one another well is to never talk about it. Just assume that people ought to get it automatically without any help. Do that, and the culture will never grow.

Within every congregation there will be people who temperamentally are not keen on the idea of sharing lives and getting involved with hard situations. There will be others who are keen to care but who see no real reason to have Jesus at the centre—in other words, a more secular model will be in their minds. For still others, there will be real questions about the place of pastoral care that have their roots in deeply held theological convictions. Leave the vision for Christ-centred care unarticulated, and such people will continue to hold those views and very little will change.

Another excellent way of ensuring that a culture does not flourish is to articulate it academically—biblically, even—but then assume that understanding the call is enough. Understanding is wonderful, but understanding in and of itself does not change lives. Even the clearest of vision statements will be rendered useless if people merely assent to it rather than participate in it. Vision needs clear outboxes for change.

The third really good way of ensuring that no one catches the vision for biblical pastoral care is to rant about it. Many of us will know the frustration that comes when people prioritise other areas of ministry at the expense of care. Some of us will know the real, sometimes devastating pain of being in a church that does not care well. It can be easy to get frustrated, even angry. It can certainly be tempting to demand change and demand it now. There are good things in being passionate about seeing a culture of care grow in the local church, but we need to be willing to show the same patience and care in the process of growing that culture as we would want to receive once that culture has been established. No one wants to follow an angry person. However, people will often follow a humble person who is willing to use the (sometimes painful) experiences they have had to envision others for something better—and do so in ways that are gentle and wise.

What might that look like?

## Communicating the vision

Any sort of vision-casting needs to begin with Scripture. Indeed, any church should be entirely sceptical of anything that has no roots (or only shallow roots) in God's word.

If you are a church leader, one option worth thinking about is to preach through Ephesians. There is so much to explore in terms of pastoral care. When preaching, it is important to keep the main thing the main thing and not twist Scripture to fulfil our agenda, but you can show how a faithful interpretation of Scripture makes a real difference in our lives today (and we will explore that more in chapter 9).

- In Ephesians 1, you could dwell on how different the lives of your church members would be if they (and you!) truly grasped how chosen, called and clean you all are. So many pastoral struggles are rooted in us believing we are unloved, messy, and without purpose. You can cast a vision for your church being a place where people are taught, reminded and encouraged to live out our true identity.
- In Ephesians 2, there is scope for exploring what it means for everyone to be valued in the body of Christ, whatever their background.
- In Ephesians 3, you can dig deep into what it would really mean to pray the prayer of verses 16-21 for one another and mean it, week by week. Too often they are verses that are simply trotted out at the end of prayer meetings, without seeing the profound richness that they contain.
- Once you reach Ephesians 4, the heights of vision-setting can be climbed. How are the pastors going to equip members for works of service in this area? What does speaking the truth in love with one another look like? How would the church change if you really were all serious about helping each other take off your old selves and put on the new, as your minds are renewed?

- Then the outworkings in Ephesians 5 and 6 are wonderful—can the church grasp the vision of a life so countercultural that holiness and beauty are on view in stunning ways? Do people understand that the armour of God is to be put on together? That the call to be faithful prayer warriors who stand firm, and persevere, is a corporate task? Along the way there are tricky passages, of course. Slavery is abhorrent, and it can be made clear that Paul is speaking into that culture, not praising it. Submission is a term that can be misunderstood by those who want to exert power in ungodly ways—the crucial difference between submission and subjugation needs to be articulated well. But throughout the letter there is wonderful material to help Christians see more clearly who they are designed to be and how God intends the church to be the place where they grow into those people. It is such an exciting book!

As well as preaching, teaching in small groups is a great way to help people catch the vision. Whether your church has a formal small-group system or not, hopefully people are meeting together around God's word outside of Sunday services. Giving them questions to discuss that are based on God's word and focused on the area of caring well can help people wrestle through God's call on their lives for themselves.

## Clarifying the vision

Wonderful though preaching is, it is not the place where every aspect of God's call can be explored. It tends to be one-way communication—preacher to congregation—and that is not enough to ensure that something this practical has been communicated well.

After the biblical material has been taught and time given to people to digest it, a vision evening can be dedicated to caring for one another. Doing something like this is an important component in helping the church know the direction for the future. This might be a dedicated evening on this topic, it might be part of your regular pattern of church meetings, or it might be a section in an annual meeting. Churches vary so much in how they function, but, hopefully, there is an obvious place in your calendar to talk about the importance of caring for each other well.

In this vision-setting evening, there can be a clear articulation of the main points. A loving church is one that is...

- rooted in God's word.
- dependent on the Lord through prayer.
- keen to love others well.
- involved in each other's lives in ways that are deep, biblical and wise.
- quick to listen to one another with humility.
- eager to pursue Christ-centred change with one another.
- willing to speak into each other's lives in ways that are truthful and lovingly gentle.
- committed to building each other up.

The precise wording can change, of course! Different churches may want to emphasise specific points because of the context they are in—but casting the vision clearly is essential.

Offering people the chance to ask questions is also important. Some will have theological questions. Some will have practical questions (hopefully many of those will be covered in the later chapters of this book). Some may be a little scared. If someone has been hurt in the past, they may be very wary of moving in a direction that they fear may involve them getting hurt again. All questions can be welcomed, and some answered to the whole church and others dealt with in a smaller one-to-one setting.

## Exploring the vision

Hearing something once or twice is rarely enough, especially if the idea requires a significant change in thinking. Helping people catch the vision through a variety of media can be helpful.

- Exploring the theology—can you write a paper on the theology of church, particularly in regard to love? Or do a series of podcasts that tackle key passages?
- Exploring the practicalities—can you encourage people to read a book together that helps them grasp the vision for care? (It could be this one!) Some options are listed at the end of this book.
- Exploring the experience—can you invite people from other churches to speak of their experience in this area? They can share what was good and what was hard about intentionally growing a culture of care.
- Exploring common objections—can you discover what the top objections to growing in sharing lives might be in your congregation? Can you address each of those in turn—biblically, sensitively, hearing the fear below the surface as well as the questions being posed? Maybe there are one or two people who think that proclamation and personal devotions should be sufficient to help people navigate life—how might you help them explore how Jesus and Paul spent time in public proclamation and personal devotion but also pursued deep sharing and conversation as well?

- Exploring the sensitive areas—while a leaning towards openness is biblical and good, there are some areas where openness is a terrible idea. If there has been abuse, there needs to be real care in who that information is shared with. There are safeguarding regulations to abide by, and sometimes not sharing widely saves lives. If someone has been badly hurt in the context of church, real nuance is needed before pursuing change.

### Compassion within the vision

A church does need to be challenged to move forward in faithfulness but not by steamrollering those who are scared. It is particularly important in this area of care that those who are struggling are treated with honour, kindness and, well, care! The Bible reminds us that the weaker brothers and sisters are to be treated with special honour (1 Corinthians 12:22-23). There should never be an attitude of "Well, they are just going to have to put up with the changes to come". That is not what treating someone with honour looks like. We listen to their worries. We seek to understand their fears. We take on board the safeguards that need to be in place if we are to avoid causing further pain. We hold their hurts tenderly and speak warmly of the way the Lord catches their tears. We move slowly, one step at a time, acknowledging that it is okay for a church to grow at a pace that is not going to wound. We speak confidently of the Lord's sustaining hand and shepherdly care when we are walking paths that feel unfamiliar and hard. We ask the question, "What would help you come on this journey with us?" We source specialist help for people if that is needed. We reinforce the principle that no one is going to be forced to share things they do not want to share. We keep checking in to find out how they are doing with the change that is taking place.

A church that is seeking to grow in its Christ-like care will need to be a church that cares well for those who do not want the church to grow in these ways. A culture of care cannot be established at the expense of those who are not on board. Individuals with reservations cannot be allowed to prevent a church from becoming more like Jesus, but every step of the way they should be loved. Doing anything else undermines the culture from day one.

## Conversations about the vision

Along the way, it is good to encourage people to be chatting about God's call in very informal ways, and we can all be involved in this. Meeting up in coffee shops, going for a walk or sitting in each other's homes and working out what the vision of Christ-centred care means for us is important. If everyone in the congregation is to really grasp what it means to play their part, they will need to think that through with their brothers and sisters in Christ. We can all be people who follow the call to "spur one another on towards love and good deeds" (Hebrews 10:24).

We can help in prioritising speaking with the Lord too. Pray with thanksgiving for those who are enthusiastic. Pray with compassion for those who are worried. Pray for wisdom for those in leadership. Pray for humility for those who are differing with one another. Pray for the Spirit to be opening God's word so people see Jesus calling them to this new, deeper way of being church. Pray for protection against the devil's schemes. Pray that the Lord will equip everyone to play their part. Pray, pray, pray—because the Lord loves to answer his children by growing them to be more like his Son.

## Vision FAQs

1. *I've just been asked: Isn't all this pastoral-care thinking just a modern fad?*
   We are talking much more about mental health these days than we did in previous decades. Mostly that is good—we are serious about helping people in need. However, the church being passionate about pastoral care is far from new. The Bible speaks clearly into anxiety, despair, grief and addiction. The early Christians wrestled with the ways in which the gospel impacted real life situations such as marriage, parenting, adoption, military service and so on. The 16th- and 17th-century Puritans were extraordinarily nuanced in the ways they talked about fear, grief, guilt and shame. Until the 20th century, it was assumed that the church was the place of pastoral care—it is only in more recent decades that much of what the church used to do has been taken on by the state. This rethinking of care in the local church, then, is not so much a novelty as it is a reclamation of what was set aside in the last century.

2. *What if I want my church to grow like this but my pastor doesn't?*
   It can be so very hard when you have caught a biblical vision for care but your pastor's priorities are elsewhere. It is worth remembering that they probably have a fuller overview of the church than you do, and so it is possible that they are quite right to say, "Not right now"—sometimes there are other pressing things going on or other/higher priorities to address. Pastors are also only human—they have limits to their capacity, and we do not want to break pastors by overburdening them. However, if they do not see the

biblical call, then that can get very tricky indeed. It is never a good idea to mount a revolution behind the leadership's back. Prayer is the best place in which to begin. Keeping the conversation live (not every week but from time to time) might provide opportunities for growth. Offer things that you could do rather than tell your pastor about things they could do. I've seen a lot of leaders change over time, but if they do not, then there are still plenty of ways you can be a godly role model, and that will impact the culture of your church for good.

## Questions for reflection

1. What part can you play in casting a vision for Christ-centred care in your church?
2. What are some of the big questions the people around you are asking? Can you make a list and begin to think of some biblical responses?
3. Who might you be tempted to steamroller in your passion for change? Pray for them now. What would it look like to love them as you pursue this change within the congregation?

## CHAPTER 8

# DIVERSITY: GROWING THROUGH USING DIFFERING GIFTS

Have you ever noticed how wonderfully gifted your brothers and sisters in Christ are? Take a moment to let your mind wander round your church family.

Who are...

- the prayer warriors?
- the wonderfully efficient administrators?
- the people who are extraordinarily gifted at listening?
- the teachers?
- the people who just roll up their sleeves and get on with all the practical tasks?
- the great cooks?
- the ones overflowing with financial wisdom?
- the ones whom people naturally turn to in times of stress?
- the ones who love to open their home to others in the church?
- the ones who love to give?

None of those people are random members of the church. Each has been hand-picked by the Father to be members of his kingdom. Each has been lovingly saved and set apart for works of service by the Son. And each has been indwelt by the Spirit and given the gifts that your church needs. Every facet of your church has been knitted together by the God who knows and loves deeply. And, if the vision we were looking at in the previous chapter is to come to pass, encouraging people to use their gifts in the service of the church in ways that honour Christ is a crucial next step.

Nothing is ever entirely easy though. Talking about gifts can be a minefield in the local church! There are (at least) three ways that the topic of gifts can trip up a local congregation.

## What gifts are not

### *1. They are not mysterious*

Many Christians are unaware of what their gifts are. In the local church, we might know that there are jobs that need doing and rotas that need filling, and there are certainly some tasks we find a little easier or more pleasurable than others, but sometimes we do not really think in terms of gifts. "I'm not teaching Sunday school because I am gifted at it," we think, "I'm doing it because it needs doing." Tasks become purely practical rather than containing a spiritual aspect. The Bible, however, shows us that God is rather more involved in the life of the local church than that.

When Jesus was describing his relationship to the church using the image of the vine and branches, he made a stark statement: "If you remain in me and I in you, you will bear much fruit; apart from me you can do nothing" (John 15:5). It's easy to gloss over the seven letters in the word "nothing", but they really are important! We can do absolutely nothing without God. That is true in the very basic sense that we cannot even breathe without him. He is intimately involved in every action that we might take, sustaining us every step of the way. But it is even more true when we look at the work of ministry. Nothing we do in the realm of sharing lives, spurring one another on to love and good works, speaking the truth in love to one another or carrying each other's burdens—none of that can happen without God equipping us to do it. It is only his astonishing generosity to the church that enables and empowers care to happen.

Within this truth—that God is equipping us to do everything that we do—we can see that some people are particularly gifted in some areas. To use more biblical language, Christ has apportioned his grace in ways which mean that some of us are wonderful teachers and others of us are able to offer hospitality and so on (Ephesians 4:7-13). Those things are specific gifts from him to us, and it is worth us being intentional about identifying what gifts he has given to each of us, not least in the area of caring for others. Why would we not want to know what gifts the King of creation has decided to pass our way?!

Such a task is done best in community. Together with wise friends, look at the gifts passages in Scripture (like Romans 12:1-8; 1 Corinthians 12 – 14 and Ephesians 4:7-12) and talk about what you see in one another. Discuss what you tend to enjoy (often, we enjoy using our gifts, though not always, of course). Ask for God's wisdom to discern what he has given and thank him for his kindness.

It is worth noting that, over time, gifts can change and grow. Sometimes we will see embryonic gifts in one another, but they still need to be developed. But once we all know what our gifts are, we are much more likely to use them. No one is intentional about using a gift they don't know they have!

### *2. They are not in a hierarchy*

Even if we know how we're gifted, we may then be ashamed or disappointed by the gifts we have received. Those words may not come out of our mouths, but, in our hearts, we can be a little negative about the gifts we have. Maybe we think the only really valuable gifts are the preaching/teaching/leading kinds of gifts. Or maybe what we would really like is one of the hotly debated gifts, like tongues or prophecy. (I am not going to get into the complexity of those in this book—maybe that is something you would like to chat over with your church leadership if you have questions.) We may know, in theory, that all gifts are precious presents from the Lord and are useful to the church, but we might actually believe that ours are not worth that much. Maybe we think that love and care can quite happily happen without whatever God has given us.

If this is how you find yourself thinking, I'd like to invite you to think for a moment about a Bible verse or passage that you find particularly encouraging—words that have done your heart much good in recent years. For me, that might be "See what great love the Father has lavished on us, that we should be called children of God! And that is what we are!" (1 John 3:1). Every time I read it, I smile—they are astonishing words.

Now, consider what gifts within the church were needed to ensure that those words in that verse or passage that you thought of reached your eyes and ears. Of course, you needed the Holy Spirit to inspire the Bible writer to write them down in the first place. But you also needed scribes who could copy them out time and time again without making any errors. You needed wise translators to get those words into a language you could understand. You needed printers, booksellers or app developers to get a Bible with those words into your hands. You needed teachers to help you understand them and get excited about them. You needed friends to share them with so they would really do their work of being something that was spoken about between believers. All those gifts played their part—some of them not particularly impressive but all of them essential.

It is the same with caring for others. Not everyone is going to give that fantastic biblical talk on anxiety. Not everyone is going to be dripping with wisdom in the pastoral complexities of helping someone navigate a tragedy. But everyone, including you, has at least one gift that is not just valuable but foundational to your church thriving. God does not gift just a few of his children with gifts needed for care, and then give the rest of his children ones that aren't really necessary, just so they have something. He is wise and kind and purposeful. And when he gave some people an ability to understand the biblical approach to walking alongside someone with bipolar disorder and another person the ability to fix printers, he did not mess up. Helping each other know that all the gifts that have been given really are important to the church is another vital step in galvanising everyone to play their part in spurring one another on to love and good works.

### *3. They are not a self-indulgence*

The gifts we are given are not really for us. They are for our church. It is possible to get a bit precious about our gifts, as if they are ours to use as we see fit. The Bible is clear that gifts are given by God for the common good (1 Corinthians 12:7), but sometimes that important point gets lost in the conversation.

There is nothing quite like a social-media meme to make me hold my head in my hands. "You do you." "Live life on your terms." "Follow your dreams." Phrases like those can sound quite affirming, but what a second-best life they lead us towards. As Christians, our calling is to do something better than "you"—we are called to be like Christ. Our *raison-d'etre* is far more exciting than "our terms"; it's living for heavenly treasure. What a blessing awaits us if we look beyond our dreams to God's extraordinary kingdom purposes. That mindset needs to frame our understanding of our gifts; otherwise we end up in the trap of thinking, “These are my gifts—I can use them how I want”. No—God’s gifts to God’s people are to build up God’s church for God’s glory.

Hopefully, we will absolutely still enjoy using our gifts—God does not call us to hate our Christian service or only use our gifts in a church context. And we retain agency about how are gifts are deployed—in a healthy church no one is forced to use their gifts, and there may well be seasons (the birth of a baby, caring for an elderly relative, personal ill health) when we simply do not have the capacity to exercise the gifts we have been given to any great extent. But our thinking about gifts will involve the concept of sacrifice—we will acknowledge that we are not at the centre of our use of our gifts; God and his church are.

## What knowing our gifts does

If you can help each other in your church know what your gifts are, each be excited about the gifts you have so generously been given, and be committed to using those gifts to the glory of God and the good of the congregation, there is an excellent chance that your church will be one where people are using their gifts well, and as that happens, the church will be built up. It is as people know God’s generosity, see their calling to respond to his generosity and see the opportunities that are there to use their gifts that they get excited about service.

All of us have a role to play in helping each other see our gifts. It can be such a blessing to give each other suggestions such as “I think you may have the spiritual gift of X” from time to time. We do not need to be in positions of leadership to be able to spot people who are gifted at hospitality, encouragement, explaining the Bible well and so on.

Leaders, however, might have a particularly strategic role in helping people develop gifts. If you are a leader, maybe you could set aside a service and a small-group session to help congregation members know what the gifts are, how they are discerned and how believers are called to respond to the gifts God gives them. Maybe you could encourage people to pray for one another and give each other (gentle) feedback about their potential giftedness in small groups of maybe three people, and to be intentional about reflecting on their own gifts.

For all of us it is good to keep remembering how different gifts can be useful in caring for others. For instance, if someone is struggling with long-term depression, then, over time, lots of people with lots of gifts can helpfully play their part. Someone able to offer hospitality might be able to welcome them for a few days of rest; someone able to offer meals may be able to lighten the burden of daily cooking; someone with a car might be able to drive them to the occasional appointment; someone with teaching gifts might be able to open Scripture with them in very accessible ways; someone with a counselling gift might be able to help them turn to the Lord in the complexities of their struggles; someone with a music gift might be able to point them to songs that will lighten their heart; someone with a DIY service gift might be able to work alongside them as they tackle the household jobs that feel too hard to face alone; someone with a gift of encouragement might be able to walk with them once a week and point them to hope… the list could go on. All these people may have a role to play in spurring that person on and helping them to persevere.

If gifts are understood well, conversations about competency can happen too. Just because someone has a gift does not mean that their gift is fully developed. Someone with a teaching gift will have areas they can teach on and areas where they maybe cannot teach yet. Someone who can speak wise words into hard situations may need to start with less complex pastoral situations. Sometimes gifts plus experience are needed before certain roles are undertaken. Someone who is gifted at encouragement and knows their Bible well is not automatically equipped to be a counsellor of someone experiencing complex trauma. God's word is perfect, of course, but our handling of it is often far from perfect, and so helping people know not just what they are gifted to do but also how well developed that gift is means people know what they are not able to do yet as well as what they are. Being aware of competency is important if a church's culture of care is to be safe.

Along the way, as gifts are discerned and encouraged, there may well need to be some conversation about training (more about that in a subsequent chapter). There will certainly need to be conversation about character—any gift can quickly turn into a useless and jarring "clanging cymbal" if it is wielded without appropriate humility and love (1 Corinthians 13:1). And there will always need to be an acknowledgement that there are some jobs that need doing whether someone thinks themselves gifted to do them or not. (I remember one Sunday morning spent removing four toilet rolls that someone had rather impressively squished into the U-bend of one of the ladies' toilets—absolutely not my gifting but essential if the preaching of God's word was not to be interrupted that Sunday!). But little by little, church members can be liberated into ministry by everyone speaking wisely about gifts.

And how beautiful it is when people are encouraged in that way. Maybe there is a potential Lydia in your church—someone with property who already enjoys giving a little bit of hospitality and who, with the appropriate encouragement to see the opportunities before them, will be willing to open their home so that many others can be spurred on in their walk with the Lord (Acts 16:15). Maybe there is a potential Barnabas in your church—someone who already encourages others a little but, with their gift pointed out, could intentionally be an encouragement to many more (Acts 4:36). Maybe there is a potential "Priscilla and Aquila" couple in your church: people who probably are not going to go into full-time ministry but who, with a bit of encouragement, will be able to speak into the lives of leaders and congregation members alike, bringing understanding and hope (Romans 16:3). God's gifts are varied and wonderful. Helping people see them and use them is transformative to a church's culture.

## When someone isn't gifted

What do we say if someone is trying to do lots of caring for others but they are really not gifted or ready for the level of care they are offering? It is never easy having conversations about this, but if you are in some form of leadership role then they are necessary if we are to ensure that people do not cause real harm in their attempts to care. These conversations are not to be rushed into, but if you know things are going astray, a gentle chat in which you thank them for their service, point out what they do well, and ask them how they think they are doing in their care of others is a good place to start. It may be that you could offer them some training which will help them care more appropriately for those around them. It may be that you will need to reflect back to them some of the ways their attempts to care have misfired. At all times, the aim needs to be to build up and not tear down, but an honest conversation, saying, "Let's think about what your gifts are and help you serve in line with those gifts more" may be vital. Often people have the insight to see that their gifts may be used better elsewhere.

Sometimes, though, people do not have that insight—they genuinely believe they are helping when they are not. Of course, if their actions are a safeguarding concern, then that needs to be handled swiftly through safeguarding processes—though still with the same ethos of love and care.

## Questions for reflection

1. Are you clear about what your gifts are? (They may have changed a bit since you last reflected on a question like this.)
2. Are there opportunities—as a church, as a small group, or as a group of friends—to mutually encourage each other with greater knowledge about your gifts? And greater wisdom on how those gifts might be used?
3. Are you able to grow your vision of how different gifts can be used in caring for others? Can you reflect on just how many—and how diverse—the gifts are that are needed if pastoral care is to work well in the local church?

# CHAPTER 9

# OPPORTUNITY: GROWING THROUGH PREACHING AND TEACHING

Much love and care takes place in quiet conversations between brothers and sisters in Christ. However, it is important not to overlook the enormous pastoral potential of the normal preaching and teaching opportunities found in the local church. Since God's word is sharper than a two-edged sword and is sufficient for life and godliness, and since it therefore changes us as we engage with it, there is great pastoral significance to the week-by-week exploration of the word as it is preached. And I imagine we can all think of examples of preaching that have been of huge comfort pastorally in what has been said or how it has been said—and of examples of preaching that have had the opposite pastoral effect, because of what has been said or how it has been said—or, of course, because of what has *not* been said.

Hopefully, you can remember a sermon during which the Lord touched your heart and enabled you to see him in ways that helped you grow in love, in trust and/or in holiness. Hopefully, you can remember times when you opened Scripture with other Christians and were stirred to praise or lament or repentance or thanksgiving.

This chapter is not about how to preach or teach in general. It's more specific than that—it's about how preaching and teaching can (among other things) be a primary means by which a congregation is cared for (whether that's publicly, in small groups or in one-to-ones).

## Invite, don't just introduce

One of the most important parts of any preaching or teaching is the start. It is not necessarily the most content-rich aspect of a teaching session, but it is the moment when people mentally engage or disengage. It is the section in which those leading can set out not just what lies ahead but why it is going to be so life-giving and encouraging to those who listen with a heart that is soft and a mind that is alert.

There are many ways to begin a sermon, talk or Bible study. You might want to remind people of the story so far; sketch in a little of the historical context; tell people the main point that is lying ahead—and all of those are wonderful things to do. But when it comes to engaging the heart, using the introduction to invite people on a journey of change can be a wonderful way to begin.

Imagine your sermon or study is on John 11. It's entirely appropriate to introduce people to the genre—to what a Gospel is; it's helpful to outline who Mary and Martha are; you could usefully outline the structure of the Gospel of John or the different aspects of Jesus' sovereignty that are displayed throughout it; if it is part of a series, you could show how this passage links to the one you looked at last week.

But what about doing this, too? Acknowledge that many in the congregation will be grieving today and many will know what it is to cry, to feel anger or to have deep questions, and many others will have friends who are in that bleak place. Say that this passage is one that invites us on a journey. It offers no simplistic answers to the problem of grief, but John invites us to walk with him and discover how a downcast heart can move towards hope—hope that is rooted in the Messiah, who is sovereign even over death. Invite your listeners to come with you on that journey: bringing their pain and desperation to, and asking their questions of, the Lord who has not forgotten them.

If you begin in this way, instantly the sermon or study will have a very different feel. It's speaking into something real and present, something painful, and it is offering something better. You won't want to start every sermon that way (that would be a little too predictable, and some passages lend themselves more to this approach than others), but sometimes the more pastoral and invitational style can help people hunger for the word to come.

## Explore, don't just explain

Once the sermon has begun, the manner in which it progresses through the passage makes a significant difference to how people respond. In the goodness of God, we are likely to achieve what we aim for when opening God's word. If our aim is to help people understand, there is a good chance that, at the end of the teaching, people will understand—but they will not necessarily be moved or changed. If our aim is to help people explore and engage with the passage for themselves, then there's a much better likelihood that at the end of the teaching people will be responding to God in exciting ways. I used to think that a talk had gone well if people could remember my four (usually alliterative) points and fed back something to me along the lines of "I really appreciated the way you explained…" Now I am much more convinced that a talk has gone well if people come up to me and say something along the lines of "When we were reflecting on verses 21 and 32, I was really struck by how I tend to keep my struggles with grief inside my head—that's so different to how Mary and Martha were willing to pour out their struggles to Jesus". Or "I've always skipped over that verse about Jesus weeping. I had just assumed he was sad about his friend dying, but to see that he is moved by the very presence of death in this world—to see his passion for conquering death and making eternal life possible—I can see that he brings greater compassion and greater hope than I had ever imagined". Or "I love that when I grieve, I don't have to do so without Jesus". Or simply "One of the things about Jesus that makes me love him is the way he cares for me in my sadness".

None of this requires being vague on exposition! God speaks clearly, and we want to reflect his clarity in the ways we teach. However, if the primary emphasis is on exploration rather than explaining, we'll include a lot more phrases like (if the passage in view is John 11)…

- "Take a moment to think about how that would feel."
- "How does that differ from how you see God right now?"
- "Would you ever speak to the Lord like that?"
- "Can you feel the depth of Jesus' compassion? Can you glimpse the power he has over death? Can you grasp the hope that he brings to you, as you mourn the one you love?"

Whether it is a sermon requiring rhetorical questions, an interactive talk where people chat to the person next to them or a small-group study that is entirely conversational, posing these reflective, exploratory questions can help people engage more deeply with the text.

## Personalise, don't just point out

On a similar note, the various ways we use subheadings in a sermon or talk (or the different ways we divide up Bible-study questions) can create very different experiences for those being taught. I remember hearing the same passage preached twice on the same day by different preachers (it was a big church, with multiple services, where the same passage ran through every service, but different speakers were tasked with proclaiming God's word). In terms of theology, both sermons were very similar, and they both had the same main points. But the way those main points were articulated on the screen were subtly but importantly different. One preacher used an accurate but impersonal voice:

- God is…
- God says…
- We respond by…

The second preacher was far more attuned to the congregation's hearts. His points were along the lines of:

- Can you see who God is?
- Can you hear his invitation to you?
- What will you do next?

The conversations after the second sermon were far more about responding to God, living for God, and loving God more in all the ups and downs of life. That's because the sermon points were not just facts—they were moments calling the people to engage with the God who treasures them. They prompted deep relational engagement rather than constituting a mere navigational or memorisation tool.

## Feel, don't just fact-find

Emotions, as we looked at earlier in this book, can have a poor reputation in the church. Sometimes they have been used to manipulate or sometimes they have been shunned as if they were evil—and so it can seem hard to include them in a talk or study without worrying that we are about to head into dangerous territory. But God is a God who feels—not capriciously but deeply. And, in his word, he gives us a rich vocabulary to express emotion. Think back to John 11 again: there is real passion in John's words as he describes the grief of Mary and Martha, of the crowd and indeed of Jesus (v 33). When Jesus expressed emotion, the crowd responded "See how he loved him" (v 36). (Or at least, some of the crowd did. Others were puzzled and possibly even angry that Jesus had not saved Lazarus earlier, v 37.) We do not have a record of the emotions expressed after Lazarus came out of the grave (v 43), but I think we can assume there was some kind of response in the people who saw Lazarus emerging, still wrapped in his graveclothes. The point is that there is an abundance of emotion there.

To be faithful to the text requires us to be faithful to the emotion of the passage. Of course, no preacher or teacher can whip up depths of grief and nor should they seek to, but the words we use to help people appreciate the passage and respond to God in light of the passage need to contain the same emotional range as the passage itself. Can we explore the experience of grief? Can we reflect on the dissonance between having big questions about why Jesus did not save earlier and still expressing trust in him? Can we wonder what would it be like to cry before Jesus as some of the crowd did? Can we describe what it is like to grieve with hope in a Saviour who has conquered death, and how different that is to other kinds of grief? I am often struck by how many Christians have no idea how to express emotions to the Lord and therefore never bring their emotions to him, so that God's word is never applied to those emotions like the powerful, comforting, healing, transforming balm that it is. In our sermons, studies and talks, we can model what it is to speak emotionally to the one who, in his time on earth, experienced emotions that were maximal and perfect and real. When we do this, we give space and opportunity for people to hear the beautiful words he says to us in our pain, and in our joy, and in the usual tangle of emotions we carry around with us.

## Abide, don't just apply

Maybe it is just me, but I think that the end of a talk or a Bible study is not a great place in which to put all the application. Everyone is starting to get tired, concentration is beginning to wane, and sometimes it's at this point that we may realise we are running out of time and we begin to cut corners, and so the application gets short-changed. Additionally, if application is in a nice, neat section of its own, it can sometimes turn into a "Here are the things I need to do" list rather than a personal, reflective turning to the Lord in worship in ways that are attentive to the nuances of the passage.

There is no hard-and-fast rule that says application needs to come at the end (honestly, I've checked). There is nothing that says application needs to be "something I must do". Periodically in the sermon or study, we can simply pause and allow people a moment to respond to the Lord. That might be out loud or it might be in the quietness of our hearts (whatever fits best in our particular setting), but it can be a way to intentionally build in moments of response.

Back to John 11: we could have a moment of silence after reading of Lazarus' death and Mary's reflections, allowing people to bring their own questions about grief to the Lord. After reading of Jesus weeping, we could encourage one another to reflect on the depth of compassion we find in Christ. After Lazarus exits the grave, we could talk about what that might have been like—what does it tell us about God's power? We can have moments of discussion at the end: on what it would look like to take a step towards trust and grieve with hope, and about how we might help each other remember, this week, that Jesus is sovereign even over death.

## Converse, don't just conclude

When it comes to sermons and Bible studies, it's great not to stop at the end. A sermon or a Bible study is a staging post in someone's journey of engaging with the passage under consideration—it is not the totality. So, to ensure that our weekly Bible-teaching is making the biggest pastoral impact it can, it's necessary to equip people to pray about what God has said to them through his word and to continue speaking about the passage with others in the church. That is, in part, what Paul encourages the Colossian church to do when he tells them to teach one another, rather than just relying on the preacher's words (Colossians 3:16).

Sometimes it helps to have the prayers of intercession after the sermon, so they can model how to pray home the words of the passage (especially if the preacher and the person leading the prayers have liaised well). Sometimes it can be useful to give people prayer points or reflection points or discussion questions, to help them join the dots between the passage and the circumstances of life. Questions that help those who are rejoicing and those who are mourning to see connections with God's word will be helpful. As they are used, congregations are spurred on to speak the truth in love to one another as they go deeper in joining up the riches of Scripture with the realities of life week by week.

## A broader lens

The main healthy nutrition of a church is best going to come via the weekly preaching and teaching that works book by book and passage by passage through Scripture. However, there is much mileage in having some topical talks along the way. While Scripture speaks richly into every pastoral situation, it is rare for a single passage to give a rounded view of a pastoral struggle, and so a whole range of Scripture will need to be explored if a topic is to be engaged with wisely and well.

For example, Matthew 6:25-34 teaches some glorious truths and provides some wonderful invitations relevant to those struggling with anxiety. It introduces us to a Father who cares and provides, it invites us to trust him, it encourages us to lift our eyes and it is packed with imagery that inspires. However, it does not give a rounded exploration of anxiety (I suspect that is not what Jesus was aiming to do), and if we give the impression that such a passage does tell us everything we need to know about anxiety, then we are likely to leave our brothers and sisters reeling rather than full of hope.

To truly grapple with anxiety, we'd need to look at Genesis 3 to see how the brokenness of the body, as well as the heart, plays a part. We'd need to wrestle with some of the longer narratives of the Bible to see how that journey from fear to trust can take a very long time. We'd need to look at the role of the church to see that overcoming any pastoral struggle is never just a matter of personal belief but of leaning on the love and support of our brothers and sisters. A topical talk enables this approach. (And, where appropriate, it also enables the gifts of others in the congregation to be used—for instance if anxiety is the topic, a contribution from a GP or a mental-health worker might be really helpful.)

Some talks might helpfully cover our call to one-anothering ministry. As saw in the previous chapter, people can only grasp a vision for speaking the truth in love to one another if they know the vision is there. Topical talks on the nature and place of pastoral care can be invaluable. And a slow walk through Ephesians 4:22-24, explaining what it really means to take off our old self and put on our new, as our minds are renewed, can help people grasp the biblical model of change and therefore engage in it with more ease.

(As an aside, another useful strategy is book groups. There are a range of good books looking at pastoral topics from a biblical perspective. Reading them as a group—perhaps by reading a chapter a month and then looking together at the reflection questions that often appear at the end of each chapter—can be a really simple yet effective way of helping one another understand, engage and grow.)

Such topical events have a range of benefits: they raise awareness of common pastoral struggles, they signal that God is not just aware of but active in those pastoral struggles, and they show that the church is a place where these things can be brought into the light and talked about together. Their existence will, little by little, help change the culture of the church—all rooted in God's word.

## Bear it in mind

As I said at the beginning, this chapter is in no way seeking to say everything necessary about preaching or teaching. My aim is more limited than that, but I think no less important: to encourage you, if you have any teaching ministry, to think about and engage with the ways a Bible passage can pastor people's hearts, so that a church's teaching becomes a key part of the way a church cares for its people.

## Questions for reflection

1. If you preach or teach, what are ways you can tweak your sermons or studies in order to engage the heart and promote engagement with God and others?
2. Next time you listen to a sermon or participate in a study, what difference might this chapter make to your mindset? How might it prompt you to speak differently with a fellow church member afterwards?
3. What are some of the most common pastoral struggles in your church? Is it possible run a topical evening or book group on that topic? Or can you meet with a friend to think biblically and pastorally about one particular struggle?

## CHAPTER 10

# EXAMPLE: GROWING THROUGH ROLE-MODELLING

Not all of us have the privilege of being involved in vision-setting or teaching—but all of us, however long we have been a Christian and whatever our role in our church, have the potential to be a role model to those around us—to be culture-setters in our congregation.

Role-modelling is something God takes very seriously. Jesus, in his earthly ministry, surrounded himself with a small group of people who not only benefited from his teaching but also were able to spend quality time with him, watching him and learning from his example. In the early church, we see that same dynamic at play. Paul took younger leaders under his wing, such as Timothy: initially giving him the privilege of shadowing him on his missionary journeys and then later, once Timothy was involved in leadership himself, keeping in touch through letters that provided much wisdom and encouragement. Indeed, the concept of Christians showing other Christians how to live for Christ is set out as part of church life. In Titus 2, Paul encourages older, more mature believers to teach younger Christians, and he says that such mentoring should include setting an example (v 7).

Anyone who has ever had any contact with children will know that they tend to emulate the significant adults in their life. There is, without doubt, a place for parents teaching their children what is good and what is not, but children often learn best by simply copying what they see happening around them. They learn by example. So do we. Words, attitudes, and actions are a little bit contagious. Culture is caught as much as it is taught.

There are ways this can be unhelpful in a church. If there is a culture of gossip or backbiting, we can find ourselves getting drawn into all kinds of ungodly and unwise conversations. Yet more positively, this contagious aspect of living life can also be a huge asset. You do not have to have a named role in the local church to be able to influence others for good. You simply need to live life in ways that shine for Jesus, and, to a certain extent at least, it will catch on. If you are praying that your actions will influence others for the glory of God and the good of the church, that's even better.

But in what ways can you be a role-model to those around? The list is almost endless, but here are four areas that might be particularly significant.

## Role-modelling countercultural love

Let's face it—there are some people who are easier to love than others. Some people have the same theological or political views as us, the same sense of humour as us, the same interests as us or the same outlook on life as us—they fit into our homes and our lives. Often they become wonderful friends, and that's great; but if we limit ourselves to only loving them, then our love is very far from the kind of love that God is calling us to.

Jesus had some stern words to say to those who only loved those who loved them back. Convenient love is not Christ-like love. Jesus wants his children to love those who are "inconvenient" (Matthew 5:43-48): those who do not love us back; those whom we have to work hard at understanding; those whose personalities or preferences grate upon us; those who are not very pleasant to us at all. If we move towards those kinds of people in love, that is when Christ is honoured. It is not easy to love like this—while it does not necessarily take more time, it will certainly take more prayerfulness and intentionality.

If you want to help your church grow in its culture of care, one wonderful way to start is to look around the congregation, spot who is a bit more lonely, a bit more quirky or a bit more spiky, and say hello. Try to chat with them after the service. Some weeks, invite them to Sunday lunch. Some weeks, offer to go for a walk with them or engage in an activity that they enjoy. Watch a sport you don't enjoy, try a hobby that does not appeal or ask about a subject that does not interest you, because, in doing so, you are taking an interest in someone in your community or church and loving them well. Often, I find that below the things that I find hard there is someone I come to enjoy loving. We are, after all, bound together by being made in the image of God and by having one Lord, one Father and one Spirit. Be known in your church as someone who displays Christ-like love and not comfortable love—and enjoy others noticing that and trying to do the same.

## Role-modelling hospitality

Allied to this is the possibility of being someone who is passionate about hospitality. Different churches will have different struggles in this area. Some churches are full of people who chat politely on a Sunday morning but never go near each other midweek. Some church members are in and out of each other's houses but only for very well-organised dinner parties where the conversation stays quite superficial. Some people are enthusiastic about meeting up in the local park (often around children's activities) but feel unable to welcome church family into their home.

Some people struggle with poor living conditions and are embarrassed to invite people round. But whatever our own church culture and our own personal circumstances, the call is to increasingly throw wide open our doors and welcome people in.

Many years ago I led a small Bible-study group for people who struggled with their English. Some of the members had lovely homes; others were living very simply. It was very easy for us to default to having social events at the homes that were larger, where the people involved had a budget that was bigger—and, to a certain extent, that did make sense. But one of my favourite memories of that group is when we all piled into the tiny bedsit of one member. There were not enough chairs for us. It was so cramped that we had to climb over each other to find a space to perch. She did not own a table, so we put our glasses on the ironing board instead. She could not afford to buy food (some of us brought small and simple things to share). All our host could offer us was a front door to walk through, an abundance of love and some tap water to drink. And it was a brilliant evening. We laughed, we shared, we prayed. That is hospitality: the act of welcoming brothers and sisters into your home and sharing what you have.

Church culture does not change overnight. You will not be able to move from zero contact to frequent hospitality, or from formal dinner parties to relaxed life-sharing, in the blink of an eye. But you can start to make progress in that direction. Suggest a simple cup of coffee together. Invite one or two people round for a light lunch. Keep the numbers small (the more people you invite, the more superficial the conversation often remains), and welcome people into your home simply with the desire to love them well. As you do so, others may catch the vision and start to do likewise.

## Role-modelling pointing to Jesus

When people share with us that life is good or life is hard, we can be diligent in helping everyone involved in the conversation lift their eyes to Jesus. That does not mean playing "spiritual snap" like Surface-level Saj in chapter 3, where we hear a key word and slap down a Bible verse that sort of fits. It does means responding to what has been shared with us in ways that are pointing to Christ.

After we have done a lot of listening, this might look like asking questions that help people relate their own story to Jesus:

> *"I'm sorry life is so complex. How can we pray about this together?"*

Sometimes, it might involve helping people lament:

> *"As you were speaking, some of the early verses of Habakkuk were springing to my mind. 'How long, Lord?' 'Why, Lord?' What questions are going through your mind? What do you want to tell God?"*

Sometimes, it might involve helping people to praise:

> *"I'm so pleased for you. What a blessing from the Lord!"*

Sometimes, it might involve helping people use biblical language to express their pain:

> *"That sounds so painful. Are there any biblical characters or experiences that are resonating right now? Job? David? Ruth? The Israelites wandering in the desert? Joseph sitting in a pit? Can any of their words be your words too?"*

Sometimes, it might involve encouragement:

*"I can see why keeping going is feeling hard. Shall we explore Psalm 23 together to remind each other of the Lord's shepherdly care in seasons like this?"*

People who are struggling do not need trite comments or mini-sermons in conversations. But small signposts to Jesus can make a world of difference.

## Role-modelling answering questions honestly

Often in books or courses on caring for others, significant attention is given to asking good questions. We have done a bit of that in this book. We can ask people how they are doing, how they are feeling, what joys and sorrows they are experiencing, what they are learning about God, how they are finding turning to God and what we can pray for them. Asking good questions is crucial. However, I find people often struggle to answer questions more than they struggle to ask them. Being people who role-model how to answer questions is a pivotal skill to master if a church culture is to grow.

Let's take the most obvious question: "How are you?" Most of us will get asked this multiple times each week. There are some moments when you will not want to answer that question deeply or in detail—you might be rushing to a meeting, or it might have been asked by someone you do not trust—in which case you can simply say, "Fine, thank you" and move on. But if you are with a brother or sister in Christ and you see an opportunity to role-model Christ-centred conversation, then avoid saying, "Fine, thank you" because that instantly closes down the conversation! Instead, you can try beginning your responses like this:

*"It's been a good week, thank you. I've been particularly encouraged by..."*

> *"Thanks for asking. It's been a hard day today. I'm grateful to God for his provision, but I'm feeling tired and a little low."*
>
> *"Thank you. I'm doing well. So much to be thankful for. I've recently been rejoicing in some answered prayer."*
>
> *"Thanks for checking in. If I'm honest, I could probably do with some prayer."*

None of those responses involve you tumbling out your deepest thoughts in a splurge. When people ask, "How are you?" they are not necessarily ready to go really deep straight away. Each of those responses, however, provides the other person with something concrete to pick up on. And that's the crucial bit about answering questions—our answers need to provide others with fuel for a follow-up question.

If your friend does not want to chat, he or she may not ask a follow-up question. That's okay. You have role-modelled answering honestly, and that is a good thing in and of itself. If your friend does want to chat, you have given them something to focus on—something that will begin to propel your conversation in a deeper rather than a more superficial direction, and that can be wonderfully fruitful. As they ask more questions, your answers can go a little deeper still, making sure you talk about your heart as well as your circumstances. You can respond with honest, open comments such as "I'm struggling with work; there is someone there I find it hard to love. I'm getting a bit tetchy, and I have noticed I am not turning to the Lord very much in the midst of the stress." Or "I'm finding parenting a joy, but I've noticed pride lurking in my heart every time my child achieves something good". Or "I'm so grateful for God's many good gifts, but I do find there is discontent in my heart when I think about..."

Not every conversation needs to go deep. There are times to chat about the football, talk about a novel or recommend a YouTube clip you've just been watching. There are times simply to laugh together. But role-modelling how to go deeper in conversations can help others see the goodness, normality and fruitfulness of aiming for more than just small talk. As we go deeper, we are able to give and receive Christ's comfort and encouragement. Showing people how to do that can have a significant impact on a church's culture.

## Role-modelling failure

When it comes to role-modelling, most of us probably want to role-model doing things well. It is quite appealing to be known as someone who role-models wisdom and love in abundance. But being able to role-model failure is pivotal too because being able to fail well is a skill that, in a fallen world, everyone needs.

I have a theory that I cannot prove, but I am fairly confident that it is right: one of the reasons why many Christians do not ask for help when a sin is "small" but only once they've reached a crisis point in their life is because most of us have absolutely no idea what to say or how to act when life is going astray. When we talk about sin and repentance in church, we often speak in very general categories; we often do not have examples of how to speak about specifics. This has been compounded by some high-profile leaders falling into sin and then, instead of repenting, engaging in what might be described as "image management"—denying wrongdoing or minimising their sins, blaming others and deriding those seeking to help people who have been wounded. If that is what is being role-modelled, it is no wonder that most people try to hide or minimise their sin rather than address it. We need to show each other better ways of dealing with our wayward hearts.

Modelling failure takes humility. It means being willing to let others see our sins, flaws and mistakes. Excitingly, it also means letting others see God's grace in technicolour and letting them be part of our wonderful story of restoration and change. Scripture is packed with examples of Christians doing just that. Paul was quite willing to be known as the "worst of sinners" (1 Timothy 1:16). We have the example of Peter denying Jesus but being restored gently by Jesus' words (John 21:15-18). We have the prayer of David, written in repentance after being confronted by his sin towards Bath-sheba (Psalm 51). It is normal for believers to sin, it should be normal for us to repent, and it is normal (though also glorious) for us to receive grace. What ought actually to be abnormal is for us to want to keep dark things in the dark, given that we follow the one who is true light. Role-modelling honesty about sin, and a response of repentance and restoration, can be wonderfully helpful to those around us.

What might that look like? It is not about telling everyone everything about your wayward heart! Rather it could mean...

- asking for prayer for your pride, your jealousy, your stubbornness, your anger, or your desire to control: "Please pray that I will find a new job—and pray that I will not envy those who are happy at work, which I'm really struggling with at the moment, but rather trust God for the future".
- initiating conversation that welcomes the topic of sin: "How is your battle for holiness going? Anything I can be praying for you in that area?" or "Would you be a prayer warrior for me as I battle with some things in my heart that are not as they should be?"

- being willing to talk about idolatry in your conversations: "I know God is calling me to trust him as King, but I see in my heart a constant pull towards seeing my security as lying in my health or family networks or high income".
- in good friendships, seeing it as normal to include times of repentance when you pray together: "Father, I'm sorry for the way I tend to use my words to try to get my children to merely comply rather than helping them grow into those children who choose to follow you".
- not being shocked if people want to talk about sin: "Thank you for sharing what is hard. I'm keen to walk alongside you in this"

Being people who are willing to be honest, willing to repent, willing to embrace grace and willing to show we believe we really are forgiven can be transformative in a church, helping others flourish and grow in its culture of care. And the great thing is that all of us, no matter who we are or how we're doing or how long we've been a Christian, can all be that kind of light to those around us.

## Questions for reflection

1. What excites you about the biblical call to be a role model? Are there any fears?
2. How might you be able to help your church grow by modelling small changes in your conversation or the way you use your home?
3. What would it look like for you to show others how to fail well? What might hold you back from helping your church grow in this area? How might you overcome those obstacles?

# CHAPTER 11

# WISDOM: GROWING THROUGH SAFE STRUCTURES AND PROCESSES

Church is a community of believers. We are bound together by God's love, and we are called to love one another. In many ways, church is designed to be like a family—a good, healthy, Christ-centred family. The relationships are designed to be deep, and they grow naturally as we keep turning to Christ. At the same time, a local church is also like a building (Ephesians 2:21), and that means there is an element of structure needed. The church is built on Christ—the cornerstone—and on Christ's word imparted to the apostles and prophets. But as we build on that, there needs to be a structure that honours Christ and enables the church to flourish faithfully in this work of caring for one another well.

The structure of pastoral care is not "one size fits all". A small church plant of twelve people will operate very differently to a huge, long-established church. A church in a place where people naturally share what is going on will need a different structure to a church where people tend to be very reticent about opening up. Some churches have elders and deacons; others do not use those terms. What follows in this chapter is not so much a "How to structure care" manual as more of a "What questions might you need to consider as you think about your care structure?" prompt.

### 1. How is your current structure working?

Find approximately five members of your congregation: one who has been there a long time and is maybe a little more mature in years, one who is relatively new but committed, one who is a young parent, one who is single, and one who is very much on the edges of church life. Try to include one person who is flourishing and one who is finding life hard. Ask them each three simple questions:

1. How do you think pastoral care works in this church?
2. If you were struggling, who (if anyone) would you speak to and what level of struggle would prompt you to have that kind of conversation?
3. What would you expect to happen after you've had that conversation?

You can approach a bigger sample if you like, but the idea is to ask a cross-section of the church how they think care operates. The answers can often be fascinating! You might find that the care of the church is flourishing and that it is doing so in the way you expected. You might find it is flourishing but actually operating very differently to how you thought it was. You might find there is confusion, or disappointment and dissatisfaction. While some of those outcomes are more comfortable than others, it is worth knowing how care is perceived and knowing where there is potential for growth.

This kind of exercise is best done by the church leadership (or certainly with their awareness), but it can also be a fruitful topic for conversation in a small group or a ministry team.

## 2. What are some of the characteristics of your church?

When thinking about the structure of care, be attentive to the kind of church you are in.

- Is your church small and organic, middle-sized and lightly structured, or large and organised?
- Do you have a proportionally large staff team, with ample capacity for caring for others, or a small staff team that relies heavily on volunteers to do pastoral work?
- Are those involved in care highly trained and able to walk alongside people in complex situations wisely, or are they very new to care and needing a lot of support and training?
- Is the church committed to one-anothering and speaking the truth in love into each other's lives, or are they far more hesitant about it?
- Are you a new church plant where everyone is happy to be flexible or a much more established church where traditions are deeply held and change is often treated with suspicion?
- Are you a growing church that is needing to find a new structure to include new people? Or are you a declining church or a church which has just been planted, which needs to readjust to a smaller size?
- Is the culture of the church one which values structure, named roles, and clarity? Or does the church have a more organic feel, with a desire to keep structure to a minimum?

Knowing where you are as church will help you think wisely about what structure might best help you all.

### 3. Who is responsible for care? Who helps?

There are so many ways that care can be seen, shared and structured. Having some structure makes the care easier to understand, easier to access and easier to ensure that it remains biblical. Here are a few examples that crop up in churches:

- *Intentional discipleship:* No one really uses the term "care" very much, but everyone is in small groups or one to ones where the Bible is opened and there's an unwritten expectation that God's word will be applied to the lives of those meeting together in ways that are loving and wise.
- *Small-group care:* This is similar to intentional discipleship, but the small-group leaders are given a specific remit for pastoral care. Alongside opening God's word, there is an expectation that the small groups will be places of care, where relationships are deep and hard things are shared together.
- *Designated support:* Intentional discipleship or small-group care might be the norm, but when life gets hard, some additional support can be offered by the church. A few people in the church are set aside for pastoral care and encouraged to meet one to one with those who are finding life hard for a season. It is all informal, and no one is claiming to be a counsellor, but there is a group of people in the church with some training who are willing to love others well.
- *Elder-led care:* The pastor is the under-shepherd under Christ, and elders share in that shepherdly care—and so elders (and sometimes their spouses) take the lead in caring for others. This might include visiting those who are struggling and intentionally praying for church members' needs as an eldership.

- *Care-team-led care:* elders and small-group leaders might be involved in care, and even spearhead the care, but there is also a care team to support those who are not in small groups or those whose struggles exceed what a small-group leader might reasonably be expected to be able to cope with. This team might have a little more training but still offer conversational care rather than anything that might approach formal counselling.
- *Every-member ministry:* Often in conjunction with one of the above systems, there may well be an expectation that everyone takes some responsibility for loving their brothers and sisters well—speaking into each other's lives.
- *Church and parachurch delegation:* One of the above structures is in place, but there is an awareness that some pastoral matters need more specialist help, so a local biblical counsellor or Christian counsellor is identified, and some people are referred on to them.
- *Church and parachurch collaboration:* One of the above structures is in place but there is an awareness that some pastoral matters could benefit from more specialist input that can complement the church's pastoral care. A local vocational biblical counsellor offers to see members of the church for counselling, and the church and counsellor liaise with one another to ensure that all pastoral care is joined up. (Note: This is always done with the permission of and in collaboration with the person seeking help—never behind their back.)

This list is not exhaustive, but it is a fairly comprehensive overview of the kinds of ways in which care is often structured. Maybe you can see within that list what your church is already doing. Maybe you can see an idea that might be more effective than your current approach in helping you care for one another well in your particular church context. The structure of care will need to morph as the church grows and changes. If you are reading this book alongside others, now might be a good moment to share with each other your ideas for how the church's care structure is working and whether it might helpfully be structured differently.

## 4. What "supervision" do those undertaking care have?

Whether they are paid or unpaid, anyone who has a named role in caring for others (be that a small-group leader, a care-team member, a designated supporter or a more formal counsellor) should have appropriate supervision. Everyone needs help to know how to navigate pastoral situations well, and everyone needs to be accountable if churches are to ensure that people do not veer off and offer care that is unwise, unbiblical or unloving. Someone who does a lot of formal counselling should have formal supervision, and someone who does a little informal care only needs a light-touch oversight. But everyone needs something.

Perhaps your small-group leaders could have occasional chats with a small-group co-ordinator who can, among other things, pray with those offering care, listen to their questions and offer ideas on how to care well. Perhaps the members of a "Care Team" could meet together regularly in groups of three or four and offer each other peer accountability, encouraging each other to walk closely with the Lord and sharing ideas on how to approach different pastoral situations with Christ-like wisdom and care. Perhaps those meeting intentionally with those who are struggling in profound ways could have oversight from an elder or staff member—someone who can love, encourage and help them in the work of caring for others. In smaller churches, perhaps the elders could meet together to encourage one another and ask each other big questions about how care is going. In tiny church plants, perhaps the pastor can link up with the sending church for this kind of oversight.

Here, too, there is no "one size fits all" approach, but, as churches, it is important to be in a situation in which anyone who is offering help knows where to get help themselves and has people praying for them regularly in their ministry.

## 5. What kind of confidentiality can you operate with?

The kind of support mentioned above requires us to grapple with an important topic—that of confidentiality. There can sometimes be a tacit pressure in churches to maintain absolute confidentiality in every circumstance. That is not healthy, wise or safe. None of us have all the wisdom needed to help a struggling brother or sister. None of us are so omnicompetent that we no longer need others to speak into our ministry activities. No church is helped if we encourage congregation members to go around caring below the radar in ways that can easily go off the rails. We need each other, and anything that might be described as pastoral care (as opposed to just friendship) should have some measure of oversight. That does not mean that people's struggles are the subject of gossip among the church—that would be hideous—but it does mean that we acknowledge that wise care involves wise community. That often comes in the form of corporate confidentiality.

What might that look like? It might mean that everyone in a named pastoral care role has an understanding that it is okay, indeed good, to talk to their "manager" about whom they are seeing and what general approach they are taking. It might mean that everyone in a peer support group has an understanding that they can share some details of who they are seeing within that limited group, to seek wisdom. It might mean that one of the elders (or the plurality of elders) will be someone with whom all pastoral situations are shared, at least in brief. Once you have clarified what is going to be shared with whom, personal information should never go beyond these clearly delineated groups without prior permission, unless there is a safeguarding concern. But corporate confidentiality allows people to share concerns with one other person or a small group of people so that care can be offered wisely and safely.

The specifics of corporate confidentiality will, again, look different from church to church. The way confidentiality operates needs to fit the structure of the church. What is non-negotiable, however, is that churches need to be upfront about the model they choose. Most people in the congregation understand the concept that those offering care will themselves need support and oversight. Most people are absolutely fine with their information flowing as long as they know where it is flowing to and are convinced that there is good reason for the flow. People will need reassuring that their information is not going to be shared needlessly or behind their back.

One question that sometimes gets asked is: what about friendship? If a friend shares something with me, do I need oversight for that? The structures and associated corporate confidentiality recommended here are for named roles (small-group leader, care-team member, pastor, and so on). Friendship does not need to be organised or overseen. But here, wisdom is still needed. If someone is facing a really tricky situation, they may need a bit more than just a friend. When someone shares a hard thing with a friend in their church, the wisest way to respond may be by saying something like "Thank you for sharing that with me. I am very willing to walk with you and pray for you in this, but is this also the time to bring in someone with responsibility for care in the church?" In that way, the friend can just be a friend, but the person in need can at least have a conversation about whether more structured help might be useful.

## 6. Do people really understand safeguarding?

It would be remiss not to include a very short section on safeguarding here. There are some things that need to be passed on even if the person involved is not keen. Here there is still a need for wise discretion, and there is never a reason to gossip, but if someone is at risk—particularly a child or a vulnerable adult—then help must be sought from the appropriate bodies.

Safeguarding training can sometimes be seen in churches as a hoop to jump through in order to get to the exciting work of ministry. Very few look forward to an evening in a church hall or in front of a screen that is focussed on safeguarding. So, just occasionally, it is worth setting aside an evening to look at the biblical basis of safeguarding and what it would look like in practice in different scenarios and track through how it actually helps. Learning to see how safeguarding really helps is a wonderful blessing to a church.

And if you are in a church (perhaps a new, small one) that does not yet have a safeguarding policy or officer in place, please bump this up your to-do list. Someone's life may rest upon it.

## 7. How will you handle it if it all goes wrong?

We have already noted that humility is vital in any culture of care—that will involve having an awareness that churches can and do cause hurt. Sometimes that hurt is serious. It is worth pondering questions such as...

- what processes are in place to welcome feedback from people when things are beginning to go astray?
- who is able to look into such feedback and take seriously concerns raised without becoming defensive?
- what does it look like in your church to admit mistakes and repent, and lament together over any pain caused?
- do the processes that exist in this realm work in both directions—both when members are hurt by leaders and when leaders are hurt by members?
- do those in named roles (paid and unpaid) have an understanding that it is better to admit fault, step down, repent and—in time, and depending on the nature of the wrongdoing—work towards restoration than it is to cover up, blame others and try to hold on to a post? (This is not a statement to assent to but a culture to actively cultivate.)
- is there precedent for people taking a break from some or all of their ministry roles because their heart has gone astray?
- is there a willingness to hear the sins of others and takes concrete action to help them change?
- is repentance and grace seen as beautiful, and "image-management" seen as the ugly ungodliness that it is, to be actively shunned?

At this informal level, processes do not need to be policies. When things are going slightly astray, the aim is that people can listen, talk, pray, take seriously the concerns of others, love well and be willing to put aside pride to love those who are feeling sore. But those things work best if they have been explicitly discussed. If this end of the spectrum is working well, fewer situations will escalate to formal procedures.

Do not assume, though, that you will never need to know what should happen at the more serious end of things going wrong:

- What grievance policy is in place?
- Who would you turn to if a complaint were lodged, for biblical, pastoral, legal and procedural advice? (That might be more than one body).
- Is there a disciplinary policy? How does church discipline workers?
- What biblical truths are going to underpin any approach to dealing with complaints?

No one wants to face the possibility of serious sin within the church, but it does happen in churches, and it could happen in yours. Being prepared helps make the church safer—and more like Christ.

## 8. How is all this communicated?

The best structure in the world will do your church no good if it is not effectively communicated. People will only be passionate about serving within that structure if they know what it is, and it will only provide safety if it is enacted. So it is wise to remind people how caring for each other works. This could be done at an annual church meeting. On your website's members page, you could have a document setting out the basic structure and approach to confidentiality. Where appropriate, in sermons, pastors could say, "If you are struggling with this, why not get in touch with..." You can help your small-group leaders, if you have them, to be clear on how they can help their group members understand the system. If you have a course or meeting before someone becomes a member, explain it there too. It does not need to be mentioned every week, but regular reminders help keep things clear.

Let's face it, structure and systems are not the most exciting aspect of building a culture of care in the local church—and structure and systems alone are not enough—but they are immeasurably useful. Finding, communicating and living out the most appropriate structure for your church will, when implemented in conjunction with deep attentiveness to relationships, help a congregation thrive.

## Questions for reflection

1. What is the current care structure of your church? What are you thankful for? What aspects of the structure might need further thought? Who might helpfully be involved in that further thinking?
2. Is confidentiality understood well in your church? If not, how might you nuance your approach?
3. Are there any areas that need greater communication? How might that communication be achieved?

## CHAPTER 12

# INTENTIONALITY: GROWING THROUGH INVITING OTHERS TO TAKE PART

Hopefully by now you are beginning to get excited about the biblical call to share lives, encourage one another, spur each other on and speak into each other's lives—that is, excited about growing a culture of care in your church. And hopefully the preceding chapters have given you ideas of things you can pray for and do in order to help that culture of care grow. So far, however, we have been looking at some of the things individuals can enact and some big-picture ideas of how to cast a vision and put in structures that will help. In this chapter, we turn our attention to the important, and more personal, matter of inviting specific people to join us in being intentional in helping our churches grow.

It would be great to think that showing the biblical basis of speaking the truth in love to one another in the local church would be enough to galvanise every member of the congregation to spring into action. But that's not how people work. Some will be instantly excited, others will be scared, and many will look around the congregation with a sense of "I guess I'm sort of happy to give it a go, but if others could give it a go before me, then that would be good". Many people (like me) would prefer it if others could do that hard work of culture change and then, once it's bedded in a bit, they will be happy to join in. All this means that helping others to join in, in manageable ways, will be key to the growth of the culture of care in your church.

### Invite them to tweak their prayers

All growth begins with God—he defines our calling and he enables our change—and so inviting people to pray differently can be a crucial first step. Earlier in the book, we looked at some ways to pray for the church. Now might be the time to drop a line to a few people in the church and ask them to pray alongside you for this Christ-centred growth. If you are a church leader, regularly ask the rest of your leadership team to be praying. (Even if one or two of them are not enthusiastic about the biblical call to share lives, asking them to pray that the Lord's will be done in this area of church life is a good thing to do.) It is good to share the prayer requests more widely too—maybe there are some people in the congregation who just love to pray, or maybe there are some housebound members of the church who would really value being asked to do something specific to help the church grow. You might, of course, want to invite the whole church to pray. If you do that, be specific about why you are asking them to pray and what kinds of things you would like them to pray about.

If you are not a church leader, you can still invite others to pray alongside you. There is no place for mounting pastoral-care revolutions in the local church, and if your church leaders are not keen on this idea, you will need to be patient. But patience does not mean passivity. There is plenty of role-modelling you can do, and asking others in the church to pray alongside you is a wise next step. No church leader is going to object to passionate prayers asking that the church will become more like the church Jesus is calling it to be. God will answer in his own good time.

If you have the privilege of leading prayers in services, you may have the scope to lead the congregation in praying differently. It would not be wise to suddenly change gear and throw in a potentially terrifying sentence asking the Lord to expose the sinful depths of everyone present! It may, however, be apt to pray that the Lord would deepen relationships within the church in ways that honour Christ, or that you will love each other as Jesus first loved us, or that the Lord would speak into your hearts when you struggle with pride/envy/discontent/etc. Always, when seeking growth, the idea is to help people take one small step towards Christ-likeness. In your prayers, you can think about what one step towards change might look like and pray in light of that. Grounding your prayers in Scripture will show their importance and faithfulness.

On a more personal level, if you are in a one-to-one Bible-reading relationship or a small group, or if you simply pray with friends or your spouse on a regular basis, you can invite the others you are praying with to try something a little different. You could say, "I am so grateful for our times of prayer—they are a real encouragement. How would you feel about going a little deeper? Rather than praying for our circumstances, how would you feel about praying for our hearts—the things we are fearing, desiring, hoping for or avoiding?" It is possible that they may say, "I don't really want to do that", and there is no need to force the issue. Many, however, will be happy to try. And then, in gentle ways, you can begin to share more of your heart with one another and pray for each other's sanctification more richly.

## Invite them to tweak their role

Everyone in a church has the potential to impact the culture for good but some people are in particular roles that are pivotal to corporate growth.

The pastors and other preachers are, in many ways, the public face of the church on Sundays. What they say and how they say it impacts the lives of all those who hear. Earlier in this book, we looked at how building a church that cares will not change the central meaning of a passage, but it might change some of the ways we invite people to respond to God in light of Scripture. Meeting with fellow preachers in the church and inviting them to consider these changes may have a profound impact on them and the congregation.

Small-group leaders can also be key people in growing this area of church life. Can you spend some time with them (if you are a pastor)—or (if you are a congregation member) just with your own small-group leader—and chat with them about the purpose and vision of the group? What is the purpose in meeting together? Is it to do a Bible study, to pray together and/or to get to know each other (all good things)? Or is it to grow to be more like Jesus, in community, as you read the Bible, pray and get to know each other? There's a subtle but important difference there. One has activities at the centre; the other has growth at the centre and sees the activities themselves as things that fuel that growth. (If you want to read more on this, I'd recommend Steve Midgley's paper *Something Worth Meeting For*. Reading that together provides much fuel for thought, prayer and discussion.) If you land in the place of thinking that small groups are primarily about growth, having some conversations with the leaders about how relationships might need to be different if that growth is to happen will be key. If God chooses to use our conversations with one another in the process of sanctification (which is why he tells us to speak the truth in love to one another), how might conversations in a group be helpfully tweaked? How might the giving and receiving of prayer requests need to change? How might the application of the Bible study be altered? Again, all this requires intentionality and inviting people to think hard and make some changes.

Another person who may have a pivotal role to play is whoever leads the sung worship on a Sunday. How songs are introduced is important. There is no merit in whipping the congregation up into a frenzy—emotionalism does churches no good at all—but helping people to express their God-given emotions... helping people to be intentionally singing to the Lord and to each other... helping people to apply the song words to what is going on in their hearts... those things can be transformational. Encouraging people to talk about the songs is a great thing to do occasionally as well. From time to time, why not challenge people to share their favourite line from a hymn or song with a friend and explain why it is so important to them? Why not ask people to reflect on the joy/sorrow/fear/discontent that is in their heart and encourage them to find a phrase in one of the songs that pours praise or comfort or hope into that situation?

Another group of people to speak with is those who take meals round to people. Most churches do this kind of thing: a new baby is born, someone has come out of hospital, or a family are moving house, and a rota is established to organise people to take round some pasta or a casserole. It is a wonderful kindness to be able to offer this kind of help. But imagine if everyone who took round a meal was also asked to identify a song or a Bible verse to accompany the meal—something that would feed the recipient's soul, not just their body. Imagine if the person taking round the meal was asked to offer prayer as well as lasagne. It is a small tweak to a simple ministry but one that can remind people that God is present and speaking, and the community around them are keen to help their faith grow, even in the tough times or changed circumstances they are walking through.

## Invite them to tweak their conversations

If we have been role-modelling Christ-like styles of relating, it is possible that our conversations with friends have already begun to deepen. However, sometimes it is useful to invite others to join in with the growth. With good friends, you may also want to invite them to try going deeper in conversation.

You could phrase it something like this: "I'm conscious that I know how you're doing at work and at parenting and I know about your hobbies—and you know how I am doing in my day-to-day life—but it occurs to me that I don't know how you are praying about those aspects of your life or how you are understanding God's word in relation to those things, and I haven't shared with you how I am joining the dots between life and Scripture either. I hope this doesn't sound odd, but I was wondering if you would be up for that kind of conversation." Or, of course, you could just start talking more about your heart and more about Jesus, and see how your friend responds.

Alternatively, you might invite a friend or a one-to-one Bible-reading partner to spend an hour with you looking at the "one-anothering" verses of the Bible. Simply look up these references:

- Love one another (John 13:34)
- Encourage one another (Hebrews 10:25)
- Forgive one another (Ephesians 4:32)
- Serve one another (Galatians 5:13)
- Carry burdens for one another (Galatians 6:2)
- Pray for one another (James 5:16)
- Spur on one another (Hebrews 10:24)
- Comfort one another (1 Thessalonians 4:13-18)
- Speak truth in love to one another (Ephesians 4:15)
- Show hospitality to one another (1 Peter 4:9)

- Bear with one another (Colossians 3:13)
- Teach and admonish one another (Colossians 3:16)

Then talk about how your relationship would be different if you took these verses to heart. There are a few nuances to note: bearing with one another does not mean ignoring serious sin; admonishing one another is not license to be mean; forgiving one another does not ignore the need for repentance. But as you explore these verses, you will find your understanding of friendship deepens.

When taking these steps, be attentive to how your friendship is going. Friendships grow best when they grow steadily rather than being dragged kicking and screaming into new territory, but sometimes a bit of intentionality can be wonderful. Little by little, we can invite a range of our friends to begin relating to us in new ways. In the end, we may find we have a handful of friends with whom we can go really deep, and a whole host of friends with whom we can get a little deeper than we are right now. If lots of people across the church do this, the potential for growth is extraordinary.

Being intentional in the way we invite people to do life—and to do ministry—differently is so important. These conversations may feel a little strange to start with, and it may well be that we are not used to speaking with others in our church in that way. And we will want to be attentive to our role when deciding whether we are the best people to have those conversations (we can all talk to our friends, but not all of us will be best placed to talk to our pastors in this way). But inviting people to something better—something beautiful—can help us move forwards together in the process of building a culture of care.

## Questions for reflection

1. Who can you invite to pray alongside you as you seek to help your church grow in this area?
2. Are there areas of church life over which you have responsibility? If so, how might you rethink that responsibility and how might you share that with others in that ministry area?
3. Who can you invite into deeper conversations?

## CHAPTER 13

# TRAINING: GROWING THROUGH SPECIFIC DEVELOPMENT OF GIFTS

The task of caring for one another in the local church is a Spirit-enabled activity. Every person in the church is loved by Jesus and indwelt by his Spirit, and so is able to take part. Listening to one another, treating each other with gentleness, praying with one another and pointing each other to the comfort, restoration and hope that Christ brings are not specialised activities—they are simply how believers are designed to do life together. However, sometimes people feel a little unsure of how to begin—they value a few pointers on how to get started. For some, the call to love one another entails a big change in how they relate to the people around them in the church, and that requires some thinking through. Some thought on how to help people access the training they need is often necessary.

Some church leaders are very gifted in this area, and others are deeply aware that they do not have the time needed to offer extensive training well. There are some "off the peg" training opportunities listed at the end of this book, but here are a couple of basic one-hour sessions that are achievable in every church and will help people develop confidence in loving others well.

## Session 1: Developing people's ability to listen together

- Introduction and opening prayer (5 minutes)

Welcome everyone to the session, encourage them to sit in pairs and say that the session is designed to be a safe place in which to learn and practise the skill of listening to one another. The things that are shared in the session are not to be repeated outside of the session (unless there are safeguarding concerns, in which case the things said will be handled sensitively and wisely and in accordance with church policy).

- What makes a good listener? (8 minutes)

Give participants 5 minutes to share what they think the characteristics of a good listener are and what makes for a poor one. Encourage them to chat in pairs or slightly larger groups, depending on what feels most comfortable, and then take some feedback from the whole group. You might like to make a note of the things people share, either on a flipchart or on an electronic whiteboard. Identify which characteristics are most dominant in the feedback.

- Jesus, the great listener (7 minutes)

Spend some time reading John 4 and discuss how the woman at the well knew that Jesus was really listening to her. At the end of this exercise, acknowledge that we do not, however, find listening easy.

- Exercise 1: Listening is hard (5 minutes)

In pairs, ask one person to speak about something that has gone on in their life in the past few days (it does not need to be anything dramatic—a journey to work or the shops is fine). Ask that person to speak about that event for one minute and ask the other person to stay silent for that time—they can nod and make facial expressions, but they are not allowed to speak. After the minute has ended, talk about what's good and what's hard about listening and being listened to. Some people will have really enjoyed listening for a minute; others will have been bursting to interrupt, and you can acknowledge the differences in the room.

- Exercise 2: Listening involves being curious (10 minutes)

The story that has been shared so far has been short and not very detailed, but it is the start of getting to know that person better. Instruct the listener to ask some simple open questions that will help the speaker to keep talking. The listener should not speak at length themselves at this point but just ask short questions. You might want to give some example questions like "What happened next?" or "How were you feeling when that was going on?" or "To what extent is that a typical event for you?" or "How did you respond to the people around you?" or "What do you think the Lord says to us in times like these?" Give people a few minutes to progress their conversation.

- Exercise 3: Listening involves making sure you understand (10 minutes)

Reflect to the whole group that none of us hear perfectly. We may hear the words people say, but we do not always catch their meaning, and therefore it is important that we check with people to ensure we have understood them. Some of the stories just shared may not have deep meaning, but they will have shown us something about the person's week—what they enjoy, what they do, what they find frustrating or what they love.

Back in pairs, encourage the listener to summarise what they have heard in just two or three sentences, and then get them to check with the speaker to see if they have heard their partner correctly. The original speaker can then affirm or amplify the listener's understanding. If there is more time, they can continue chatting about the same topic.

- Exercise 4: Listening with a lens (10 minutes)

Explain that in most stories there are things that are good (for which we can praise God), things that are hard (which require God's comfort), and things that are wrong (for which we need grace). Those things will not be present in equal measure in every conversation, and we do not need to comment on each of them in every conversation, but listening out for each of those categories helps us listen well. Encourage people, in their pairs, to reflect on the conversation so far and talk about what reasons there are to praise God and/or what need there is for God's compassion. It is permissible to talk about things that are wrong too, but this aspect may not be present in the story shared and, even if it is, this may well not be the moment to address it—this is a practice session between people who are simply sitting next to each other, and they may not trust each other well enough to talk about the really hard things of life.

- Conclusion and closing prayer (5 minutes)

Repeat the idea that to listen well, we will want to speak little, ask good questions, check we understand and be attentive to what is worth celebrating and what is hard (as well as what is going astray). Reiterate that stories shared in the session are not to be shared more widely. Encourage people to put their listening skills into action this week and then ask for God's help to do just that.

If you extend the session to 90 minutes, there is scope for both people to practise the listening skills, not just one, by repeating Exercises 1-3 and swapping roles.

## Session 2: Developing people's ability to pray together

- Introduction and opening prayer (5 minutes)

Welcome everyone to the session, encourage them to sit in pairs and say that the session is designed to be a safe place to learn and practise the skill of praying with one another. The things that are shared in the session are not to be repeated outside of the session (unless there are safeguarding concerns in which case the things said will be handled sensitively and wisely and in accordance with church policy). Ask for God's help to pray together well.

- Praying to the God we know (10 minutes)

Spend a few moments reminding those present that prayer is a privilege and a deeply personal way to engage with the God who treasures us and loves to hear our voices. Read Ephesians 3:14-21 and talk about what that passage shows us about God, about ourselves and about how we pray to him.

- Praying wisely (8 minutes)

In the whole group, ask people to share what is useful and what is not useful when others pray for them: that is, what character traits, tone of voice, setting, content of prayers and so on are helpful or unhelpful. Draw out the reality that it is not useful when people try to impose their prayer priorities on to others (praying for things that the recipient does not want prayed for). And it is not kind to pray very personal prayers in very public settings. We want our praying to be biblical, safe and gentle. Add that it is good to pray for things that go beyond circumstances and that attend to our hearts—for instance, rather than just praying that God would provide someone with a new job, we can pray that they would have patience, trust, contentment and a deep desire to honour their current colleagues well as they seek a new job.

- Exercise 1: Praying with people we know (12 minutes)

In order to pray well with and for people, we need to know them. Generic prayers ("Lord, please grow them") have their place, but it's far better to be specific. In pairs, encourage people to spend 10 minutes chatting with each other about their day. They can put into practice some of the skills they learned in the previous listening session if they have been to that—but here, the idea is that both people share a little about their life.

- Exercise 2: Praying for the people we know (10 minutes)

In pairs, encourage people to share how they would like the other person to pray for them. Encourage people to refer back to Ephesians 3:14-21 to get some ideas of how to pray (they may also choose to refer to passages of Scripture they have read recently to get some other ideas of how to pray biblically in this area, and that is great!). Encourage people to be really specific and biblical about how they ask others to pray.

- Exercise 3: Praying in ways that are biblical and personal (10 minutes)

In pairs, encourage people to spend 10 minutes praying for each other in the ways they have identified. If there is time, it would be great for people to share within their pairs what they found particularly helpful about the prayers of the other person.

- Conclusion and closing prayer (5 minutes)

Repeat the point that to pray well, we need to know God, know others, know their needs (both circumstances and heart) and pray in ways that are biblical and personal. Reiterate that stories shared in the session are not to be shared more widely. Encourage people to put their praying skills into action this week and then ask for God's help to do just that.

## Advanced training

These two sessions are for everyone in a church. At the other end of the spectrum, some people will display exceptional skill in this area of caring for others, and they may be gifted for walking alongside people in the more complex areas of suffering. This does require some significant training if pastoral errors are to be avoided. When someone has suffered abuse or trauma, or is ensnared by multiple addictions or is facing debt problems, they can still benefit from the general encouragement, love and prayer that anyone wise in the congregation can offer, but there will also be a need for more nuanced support and formal counselling. Not everyone in the congregation is equipped to understand these kinds of pastoral complexities.

If there is someone in your church who loves Jesus, displays consistent humility, has a good understanding of how the Bible applies to the complexities of life, is diligent in prayer and is the kind of person that people naturally turn to when life is hard, then they might be the person to invest in. (Maybe that person is you.) Some conversation with them would be necessary to discern whether they have a heart for this kind of work and whether they have the capacity to train for more specialised ministry in this area—but if they are keen, helping them develop will be a privilege and of real benefit for the church.

It is often best to start slowly: perhaps by encouraging them to read a book on pastoral care with another mature individual from the church or to engage in one of the short courses listed at the end of the book. If that goes well, encouraging them to enrol on a course in conversational ministry, pastoral care or counselling may be a great next step. There is a range of courses available, and it is worth discerning which would fit best with the theological convictions of your church. Some courses are based on psychology; others are largely psychological but include small or significant elements of faith (these are often termed "integrative"); still others are primarily biblical but still aware of the insights that psychology can bring. Picking a course that equips people to serve in a way that is consistent with the wider church culture is key.

If your church is really invested in helping people grow and you are able to do so, consider using church finances to fund such a course and liberate people from other church responsibilities so they have the time to engage in such a course. And cast a vision for how the person may be able to serve (with appropriate support structures in place) if they continue to thrive in this area.

Whether someone is struggling to get off the starting blocks or they are keen to serve in more specialist ways, structured training events and pathways can be a wonderful way to help them and the wider church grow a Christ-centred culture of care.

## Questions for reflection

1. What further training might be helpful to you?
2. Who else in your church might appreciate basic or more advanced training?
3. How could you make it easier for yourself/them to access that training?

CHAPTER 14

# TESTIMONY: GROWING BY SHARING WHAT THE LORD HAS DONE

God is at work. He never falls asleep or abandons his post as the King of all things (Psalm 121:3-4). He loves to bring to pass his good purposes, and that means we can all be confident that God is going to be at work helping church members to love each other well (Philippians 1:6). So one wonderfully encouraging thing that churches can champion and make room for as they seek to grow a culture of Christ-centred care is to share testimonies of how the Lord has been growing and changing both individuals and the whole community. Testimonies are not about showcasing the gifts or godliness of specific people but are about pointing to the Lord and saying, with confidence, "He is good, and he is at work—let's keep on trusting him".

## Testimonies of lives changed

One of the reasons that I am so passionate about seeing God's word applied to the hearts of individuals in the context of the local church is that I have known the difference God's word has made to me. As I look back on my life, with the many joys and many sadnesses it has contained, I can say without any hesitation that I have changed the most when I have been diligent in turning to God, through his word and prayer, and have welcomed my brothers and sisters to speak into my heart. I love the fact that God has taken me from being someone who used to panic at the thought of booking a plane ticket to someone who really enjoys (at least short) flights when there is a reason to go abroad. I love the fact that God has taken me from being someone who struggled with nightmares to someone who usually sleeps very soundly. I love the fact that God has taken me from being someone who wanted to hide when life was hard to someone who wants to walk this life, including the hard seasons, with my brothers and sisters in Christ, not sorted-out but now surrounded by encouragement and hope. He has changed my hurting, wayward heart in so many beautiful ways. There is plenty left for him to change—I continue to struggle so much—but I can, with ease, echo the words of the psalmist who said, "I will sing the LORD's praise, for he has been good to me" (Psalm 13:6).

How about you? What are the wonderful ways in which the Lord has changed you? What about your friends or your small-group members—when was the last time you asked them how the Lord has been changing them? Or, if you lead services, when was the last time you gave someone an opportunity to share how the Lord has been working in them? It is not just the "I once was lost, but now I'm found" testimonies that are good (glorious though such stories of salvation are); it is also the stories of "I didn't know how to live for Christ in this area of my life, but now I am starting to see how to be faithful each day" or "I used to struggle a lot with this, but God is enabling me to change" that can spur on fellow believers (and indeed inspire unbelievers) to look to Christ.

Why not plan a testimony evening, whether that's a handful of people giving testimony to the whole church or a small group exchanging testimonies with one another over desserts, or just a few friends gathered in a coffee shop to encourage one another? Give each other about ten minutes (it can be longer or shorter depending on the setting) and encourage each other to share...

- how life used to be
- how God spoke to you through his word and his people—if there is a specific verse, it is good to read it out
- how you responded to God
- how you changed as a result
- what you want to praise or thank God for

They do not need to be spectacular stories: little glimpses of hope and small moments of thanksgiving can be immeasurably encouraging. Are you a little more patient with your spouse? A little more encouraging of your children? A tiny bit more content at work? A bit more passionate about prayer? Are you starting to see the joy of your salvation more clearly? Are you beginning to break free from that besetting sin that has been dragging you down for years? Is there now a little glimmer of hope in an intractable situation? Share it, praise God for it and encourage others with it. We all need reminding every day that there is no situation beyond God's redeeming care and no person who has fallen away from his sight.

## Testimonies of groups changed

It is not just individuals in whom God works. In our individualistic society, we can often think about God working in us as discrete people who just happen to share lives with one another, but he is actually very invested in us as a community. That means there will often be scope for praising God for his work in a community as a whole.

I have mentioned before a Bible-study group I used to lead. They were (and indeed are) wonderful saints. But when we started, we were just all about understanding the

Bible. As people who spoke a variety of languages, we often struggled with the basics of understanding, and that took up a lot of our time. However, over the years, as we got to know each other more and got to see the wonders of God in his word more, we became more of a community, living for Jesus together. We were never perfect, but we were able to pray for each other, spur each other on with Bible verses, take meals to one another, pay for each other's English lessons (at least in part), help each other fill out forms and so much more. We were able to share the ups and downs of life and constantly remind each other that God is good and he can be trusted in all things. We changed from being a group of people studying God's word to a group of people committed to helping each other live for God in the light of his word. Sharing that journey with others was almost as encouraging as living that journey with the group members.

So ask yourself:

- What groups are you involved with? A team serving tea and coffee? A music group? A children's work team? A small group? A prayer triplet? A friendship group?
- What has the Lord been doing in your group?
- How has he deepened your relationships?
- How has he changed the way you pray for one another?
- How has he enabled you to serve one another?
- How has the way you speak together deepened?
- As you look back over the past year or five, how has the group changed? What encouragements have you noticed? Who can you share that with?

It is important not to share other people's personal stories without their express permission, but what big-picture encouragements can you pass on to your church leadership or friends or wider church? If God is at work, let's not leave his work unacknowledged but celebrate it in church meetings or elders' meetings or over a quiet cup of coffee. It is so encouraging to see God growing groups of people.

## Testimonies of whole churches changed

As well as looking at individual and small-group growth, there will be moments to stop and think about whole-church growth. In the short letter of 3 John, the apostle John declares that he has no greater joy than to hear that his children are walking in the truth (v 4) and that he has heard great testimony about their love (v 6). Their corporate reputation was wonderful (though not without its problems), and he reflected that back to them. Even Paul's first letter to the church in Corinth, a church with a huge number of issues and challenges, includes a corporate encouragement (1 Corinthians 1:4-7)!

Periodically—maybe annually—it is no bad idea to stop and take stock of the church as a whole. There will be some discouragements (there always are), but hopefully, as you look back, you will be able to see a church that joins the dots of Scripture and the realities of life more easily. Or a church that prays together more naturally. Or a church where sins are not covered up so much, so that strugglers can be helped in the early stages rather than waiting for crises to erupt. Or a church that is getting noticed in the wider community for the incredibly countercultural and kind ways it walks alongside those facing debt. What would it look like for you (in conjunction with your church leadership if you are not a leader yourself) to review the past year or two and identify a handful of ways the church has grown, and then share and celebrate and thank God for that?

The sharing of such testimony should never give the impression that there are no problems in a church or that caring well for each other is now entirely sorted. That will never be the case. There will always be areas that need addressing. There will always be people who somehow fell through the net despite people's good intentions. There will always be things to repent of and grow in. But that does not deny that there will also be many reasons to thank the Lord for making your church even more beautiful than it was before. Take time to take stock.

## Particular callings

It may be that, as you give thanks for the people who have changed and the groups that have changed and the changes in the wider church, you begin to see some trends. It is possible that God might be giving your church, or a section of your church, a particular passion for certain people groups or for people with certain struggles. This will not always be the case, but sometimes God seems to collect people with a similar vision in the same place and set them aside for a particular work.

Not every church or group of churches needs specific ministries but, where there are possibilities, such ministries can be wonderful ways to nurture believers in distress or reach out to unbelievers facing particular hardships. What might those projects include?

- A biblical counselling ministry serving local churches
- A crisis pregnancy centre
- A debt advice centre
- An addictions ministry
- A bereavement group
- A single and lone parents' support group
- A support group for those caring for elderly relatives
- A group for those who want to discuss faith and neurodivergence

- A carers' group
- A discussion group for divorced Christians
- A safe space for those recovering from domestic abuse
- A network for those living with chronic illness or disability
- An accountability group for those seeking to break free from pornography
- An adoption and fostering support group
- A network for those serving in the armed forces—and their families
- A friendship group for international students struggling with their mental health
- A ministry to the local street population
- An outreach to sex workers in the area
- An outreach to asylum seekers—or a Bible-study group in a language other than English
- An outreach to local gang members—or knife-crime awareness
- A prison ministry or post-prison support group

The list of possibilities is almost endless, and no church will ever be in a position to address every need, but it is worth prayerfully discerning if the Lord is putting any such specialisms on the corporate heart of your church. These three questions might be a good starting point for thinking that through:

- As we listen to the testimonies of church members, are there common themes? Is God bringing along a significant number of people in specific circumstances for us to love?
- As we listen to the testimonies of church members, are there common desires? Do people want to use their experiences of God's comfort to comfort others in particular and similar ways?

- As we look at our local community, are there specific needs that we as a church (or in conjunction with other local churches) might be able to meet in a Christ-centred way?

Serving in any of these more specialised areas will need prayer, thought, planning and the wisdom of others who have gone before. With appropriate care and wise partnership, there is a whole host of ways we can honour Christ with our care to specific groups of people.

Being attentive to all that the Lord is doing is wonderfully encouraging, a great spur to continued growth, an opportunity for much praise and also a chance to take stock and discern where the Lord may be leading next. And we can all play our part in speaking of the goodness of God and encouraging others in this way.

## Questions for reflection

1. How has the Lord been changing you in recent years? What character traits or behaviours have changed to cause you to be more like Christ? With whom can you share God's kindness to you?
2. How has the Lord been at work in your relationships/groups? Can you set aside some time to encourage one another in all that the Lord has been doing?
3. Are there any particular opportunities or trends for you and the wider church to be alert to? Who can you talk to about how to serve well any people groups that you have identified?

# CONCLUSION: CONTINUING TO GROW

If you have reached this point in the book, I hope you fit into one of these two categories:

1. You are really excited and keen to get going.
2. You are really excited but feeling a little overwhelmed.

So, as we finish, it's worth asking: *What will I do next?*

## Excited and keen

I remember when I first started to read and think in this area of growing a culture of care. It was a season when I was able to reflect afresh on what God had done in my life and pair that with the biblical call to one-another, and I got very excited indeed. What potential there is for our churches to become places of Christ-honouring care: care that leads to right worship, gospel living, deep community, biblical understanding of our struggles, grace-infused conversations, passionate prayer and lives changed! Once you taste the beauty of that vision, it is easy to want to press full steam ahead. Right? Well, maybe.

I do indeed hope and pray that you are excited by what you have read. And, if you are already seeing tangible next steps falling into place, praise the Lord. May he lead you rightly through the years ahead as you seek to honour him with your life and ministry. But a word of caution: please move slowly. When I first saw the call to care and the wonder of conversational ministry, there was a season when I became more than a little insufferable! Anyone who knows me will tell you that I am an activist. There is little that I find harder than sitting still, I have 17 ideas before breakfast most days, and I long to enact at least 12. Excitement is a gift, but it can also scare the people around you. Maybe they are a little further back in the journey of wanting the help the church grow. Maybe they are a little less sure of the biblical call. Maybe they are in a season when life is already feeling a bit too overcrowded. As an act of love and care to those around, move slowly, collaboratively and kindly. The gospel is never commended by acting like a steamroller or a bull in a china shop. Pour your energy into prayer (that is where it will be most effective anyway). Take time to share some of your thoughts with those around you—maybe read this book with one or two other people—and then start chatting about what the next step for you and the wider church might be. The passion you are feeling is a joy, and make it your aim to do everything you can to ensure others experience it as a joy too.

## Excited and overwhelmed

If you have caught the vision but are feeling a little overwhelmed by what might lie ahead, please do not panic. I am probably only going to write one book on this topic, so I put quite a lot in here! However, the whole book does not need to be put into action in your church this week, or even this year.

Talk about what you have been reading with wise and godly friends. Prayerfully discern one or two steps to take and be content with that for now. There is no harm in plotting out a 5-year plan or writing a biblical list of hopes and dreams, but you can walk this path slowly. God usually changes us (and our churches) one step at a time, over a period of time. Unless there is something going on in your church that is causing actual harm to people, you have plenty of time to address the areas that need addressing. And, every step of the way, the Lord will be enabling you.

## How it looks

There is no one-size-fits-all approach to pastoral care. It will look very different in different churches. But, with Christ at the centre and the good of the church as your aim, there is no reason to think that anything in this book is unachievable. I have tried to write it in such a way that it is eminently achievable.

And that has been my experience as I have seen different churches change over the years. Here are three.

## A small church plant

The church was only a year old. It was tiny but growing and had already embedded some wonderful patterns of care. An open discussion time after the sermon encouraged people to talk about how Scripture was going to make a difference to life, and the pastor welcomed questions of all kinds. The church started an intentional drive to help people discern their gifts and use them in the service of the Lord, and that helped avoid the trap of many church plants where everyone does everything just because people are short on the ground. An ethos of one-to-one relationships that included Bible reading, prayer and mentoring deepened relationships and provided plenty of scope for people to ask big questions about the hard things in life in an environment that sought to be safe and welcoming. In human terms, it probably won't go down in history as a super-successful church plant, but the people who were in it grew significantly and loved one another well.

### The large, well-established church

The church had always had a passion for evangelism, and the Lord blessed the people there through new conversions. It was an exciting time but one that came with its problems because, as the church grew, relationships became more superficial and what had once been a rich community became more like an organisation bound together by the love of good preaching. Little by little a new structure was formed. Someone was appointed to oversee pastoral care, people were trained, the large congregation was subdivided into smaller groups where people could receive care, and a relationship was built with a local biblical counsellor who could walk alongside those facing more complex issues. Gradually the shift back to Christ-centred community began to take place. As that happened, as people were loved and encouraged well, people became even more passionate about mission, and the church grew even more.

### A tiny socioeconomically deprived church

It had been limping along for years, with good preaching and fervent evangelism but a congregation that was small and contained a disproportionately high number of people with limiting health conditions. People were hungry for real heart growth though, and so training was put on. One of the elders set aside one Saturday morning a month to help the women of the church grow in their Bible handling and pastoral care. Soon the men, including those with very few educational qualifications, were being mentored in how to read the Bible with others to promote understanding, faith and trust. The church stayed small, but the maturity of those who were a part of it grew exponentially.

No book can predict where the Lord will lead the church you are in over the years ahead. There may be struggle and challenge or there may be thriving and growth, but if you commit to caring for one another as God calls you to, there is every reason to hope that in the good times and the hard, you will all grow to be more like Christ as individuals and as a church. And, as you do so, you will grow to love one another more and love being with one another more, and others will see that too:

> *"A new command I give you: love one another. As I have loved you, so you must love one another. By this everyone will know that you are my disciples, if you love one another." (John 13:34)*

## Questions for reflection

1. How has this book impacted you?
2. What one step can you take as a result of your reading?
3. What are you looking forward to the Lord doing in you—and your church—in the years ahead?

# FURTHER READING

*Real Change* by Andrew Nicholls and Helen Thorne-Allenson (New Growth Press, 2018)

*Mental Health and Your Church* by Steve Midgley and Helen Thorne-Allenson (The Good Book Company, 2023)

*Side by Side* by Edward Welch (Crossway, 2015)

*Caring for One Another* by Edward Welch (Crossway, 2018)

*Care* by Dwayne Bond (The Good Book Company, 2025)

## Further training

Crosslands Training: Foundation Course in Pastoral Care

BCUK: The Bible and Pastoral Care

BCUK: Certificate in Conversational Ministry

Westminster Theological Seminary: Masters in Biblical Counseling

At The Good Book Company we are dedicated to helping Christians and local churches grow. We believe that God's growth process always starts with hearing clearly what he has said to us through his timeless and flawless word—the Bible.

Ever since we opened our doors in 1991, we have been striving to produce resources that are biblical, relevant, and accessible. By God's grace, we have grown to become an international publisher, encouraging ordinary Christians of every age and stage and every background and denomination to live for Christ day by day and equipping churches to grow in their knowledge of God, their love for one another, and the effectiveness of their outreach.

Call one of our friendly team for a discussion of your needs or visit one of our local websites for more information on the resources and services we provide.

Your friends at The Good Book Company